Mother and Baby
Working in Harmony

Julie Jarrett

First published 2022

Text copyright © Julie Jarrett 2022
The moral right of the author has been asserted

All rights reserved. No part of this publication may be reproduced, stored in a retrieval system, or transmitted in any form or by any means, electronic, mechanical, photocopying, recording or otherwise, without the prior written permission of the publisher and copyright holder.

A self published title
Designed and produced by Adala Publishing
www.adala.com.au

 A catalogue record for this book is available from the National Library of Australia

ISBN: 978-0-646-85971-2 (Print)
ISBN: 978-0-646-85972-9 (eBook)

Chapters and Contents

Introduction	1
A Poem From a Mother to Her Baby	7
Becoming a Parent	9
Becoming a Parent: A Changing Role for You and Your Partner	9
For the Woman	9
Preparation and Ideas for Parenting	10
For the Man	11
Becoming a Father: Phil	13
Are We on the Same Page? An Exercise for You and Your Partner	16
You, Your Partner and Your Relationship	20
You, Your Partner – Financial and Other Considerations	22
The Practical Stuff	26
A List of Essentials for Your Baby	26
Nappy Changing	27

Bathing Tips	30
Baby Soaps and Shampoos	31
Prams	32
Baby Car Seats	33
Thermometers and Fevers	33
Gifts to Give or Receive for a New Baby	35
Baby Gifts	36
Other Practical Helpful Ideas	37

The Health and Vitality of the New Mother — 39

The Kitchen	40
Enzymes	40
Food Preparation Made Easy	42
Fruit	43
Healthy Snack Ideas	44
Water	44
Setting Yourself Up for Success	48
Listening to Your Body	49
Exercising	50
Stress	51
Sleep	52

Breastfeeding Your Baby — 54

Understanding Breastfeeding and Being Change Makers	55
Finding Solutions	63
Before the Baby Arrives	65
Expressing Colostrum	65
Hand Expressing Technique	66
When Your Baby is Born	68

Ongoing Breastfeeding	71
Further Information for Breastfeeding	74
Baby Language and Feeding Cues	74
Easy Ways to Understand Breastfeeding Techniques	74
Other Positions	83
More Helpful Information for Breastfeeding	85
Change the Baby, Change the Hair Tie	87
Burping Your Baby	87
How Much Milk?	90
How Long to Breast Feed For?	91
Should my Baby be Fed on a Schedule or Demand Fed?	92
When Breastmilk is Unable to Meet the Needs of Your Baby	93
Some Considerations of Vitamins and Minerals for Mother and Baby Health	96
Your Baby's Healthy Immune System	**103**
Understanding Your Baby's Immune System	104
Developing a Deep Connection with Your Baby	**110**
Conscious Parenting	113
Carrying our Babies	114
Social Expectations	116
The Power of the Sound	118
The Power of Human Touch	118
Your Sleeping Baby	**122**
The Sleeping Space	128
Sleep Deprivation for the Parents and How to Manage	129

The Unsettled Baby	**132**
Reflux	138
Emotional Health	**143**
Overall Health, a Good Place to Start	143
A Commitment to Parenting	**149**
Assisting the Environment	**152**
Your Home	152
Shopping	154
Setting Up a Room For Your Baby	155
Baby Furniture	156
The Nappy Revolution	157
Commercial Baby Wipes	160
Bringing it all Together	**162**
Acknowledgements	**169**
References, Resources and Insightful Information	**172**
Affirmations	172
Repeat These Each Day	172
Aromatherapy Oils	173
Baby Products	173
Birth Information	173
Delayed Cord Clamping	173
Breastfeeding	174
Conscious Parenting	174
Environment	174
Emotional Health	175
Fevers in Children	175

Gut Health	175
Health Outcomes	176
Immune System	176
Magnesium	176
Nurturing from Conception	176
Safe Sleeping	177
Vitamins and Minerals	177
Vitamin K	178

Introduction

WE PUT SO MUCH energy into learning about the birth process before we have a baby, but not necessarily what is beyond birth. I have had many discussions with families and friends, who state, "I wish I had known more about what happens after I had my baby." Women, and parents to be, often gain information about the pregnancy and birth, but that is where the information stops.

When information is passed on from well-meaning family and friends it can be quite negative. Often people want to tell you their story about their baby experience. For example, how their baby kept them up all night, or vomited all over them after a feed, or how terrible it was changing nappies! The focus is often on the negative, rather than the many beautiful encounters with their baby, that occur most of the time. Those moments when you were up in the early hours of the morning feeding your baby and looking down into their eyes with an overwhelming and amazing feeling of love. We rarely hear those beautiful stories or about those special moments.

Consequently, when women are deciding to have a baby, with all these negative thoughts spoken to them, this becomes their perceived experience. They believe that when they have a baby it's going to be difficult. Having a baby and being with a baby at home can be challenging, but there is so much more that is not.

I started writing this book in very interesting times. It was April 2020, and we were in the midst of a lockdown, during a worldwide pandemic. It created difficulties for a lot of people, whilst for many others, it created opportunities to slow down and reflect on life.

Personally, it gave me the time to sit down and create this book. A project that has been dear to my heart for many years.

I became a midwife after spending time as a general nurse in a maternity ward as part of my nursing training. Times were rapidly changing, and hospitals and nurses were coming out of an era of being strictly regulated as to what they could and could not do. Women were finding their voice and being given more opportunities. The year I started my nursing training was the first year that nursing commenced in universities as a degree. I am very grateful that I did my training through the hospital system as it would take many years for the degree course to become what it is today. My hospital training, even though it was far from perfect, was life changing in many ways for me, a quiet girl from the suburbs of Melbourne.

Our group of 84 nursing students shared many experiences together and, looking back now, I understand that it was my first experience of what I now called 'sisterhood'. We shared our experiences and supported each other through difficult times.

As a nursing student, off to the maternity ward I went. As the first group of students to have set foot into this maternity ward at a major public hospital, the midwives working there were not overly pleased at having students in their 'territory'. I am sure they had to make many adjustments to have us there. It was a difficult and daunting time as a student nurse; however, I remember those first births I witnessed so well. How amazed I felt in that moment when a new life emerged into the world, in my presence. What a privilege this felt to me! It encouraged me to pursue midwifery as my future career path.

Several years later, I found myself in a large city maternity hospital, embarking on a year of study and practical experience to become a midwife. It was the beginning of a remarkable career I feel blessed to have experienced.

Through the late 70's and early 80's, many changes in society were mirrored by an increase in choices available to expectant women. Women were becoming more empowered and vocal about their rights. Birthing centres were becoming part of the landscape for earthy, radical women, who were no longer content to give their power away to doctors and midwives, who followed the traditional, medical model of birth. There was a push against the tide of companies promoting artificial feeding along with inadequate training of breastfeeding skills, to both healthcare professionals and mothers alike. Everyday women started to see the benefits of breastfeeding and were motivated to want to do it. These changes came especially from women themselves, through organisations such as the Nursing Mother's Association (now called the Australian Breastfeeding Association). Mothers motivating other mothers.

Many changes had taken place in such a short period of history. My understanding of birth and what follows birth grew after I had my own two children. It was a beautiful time of learning about the love for a child and all that goes with it.

Today in my midwifery practice, as a Lactation Consultant, I meet and care for many amazing women and their partners. Each family helps me shape the way I practise my midwifery skills. I would especially like to thank the women I have cared for who have shared their experiences with me.

Particularly memorable were my communications with the women who had completed a Hypnobirthing course. I recognised the vast difference in their wisdom, calmness, and strength of presence when they were birthing their babies. Having gained insights from these women, I decided I wanted to do further study in this field of expertise. After much research, I enrolled in the Hypnobirthing Australia course. I was impressed with the philosophies of this company. Even though I had been a qualified midwife for a long period of time by then, I learnt so much during the course. The feedback I have obtained from the women and their partners I have since taught the Hypnobirthing course to, has been amazing.

I also had the opportunity to work with a Lactation Consultant on several occasions. The beautiful and inspiring work she did with women encouraged me to go back to studying to become a Lactation Consultant. This course, and commencing in this field, have further expanded my knowledge. I am incredibly grateful for all these opportunities.

I have had an amazing journey so far. In writing this book, my hope is that women and their partners will find a common-sense approach, as well as intuitive, loving guidance for becoming parents and parenting.

This is not a textbook full of technical information, but a journey of knowledge. I have incorporated stories into the text throughout the book. The indigenous cultures in the world share information down through their generations. It is something that we have lost touch with in the modern world. Through story, we can learn a special truth by observing life through other people's eyes. We can pick out the message that is needed for us at a particular time in our lives, or we can just embrace the story for what it is.

So, enjoy the journey.

Julie Jarrett
Registered Nurse (RN) Registered Midwife (RM)
Lactation Consultant IBCLC
Childbirth Educator (CBE)
Hypnobirthing Australia Certified Practitioner

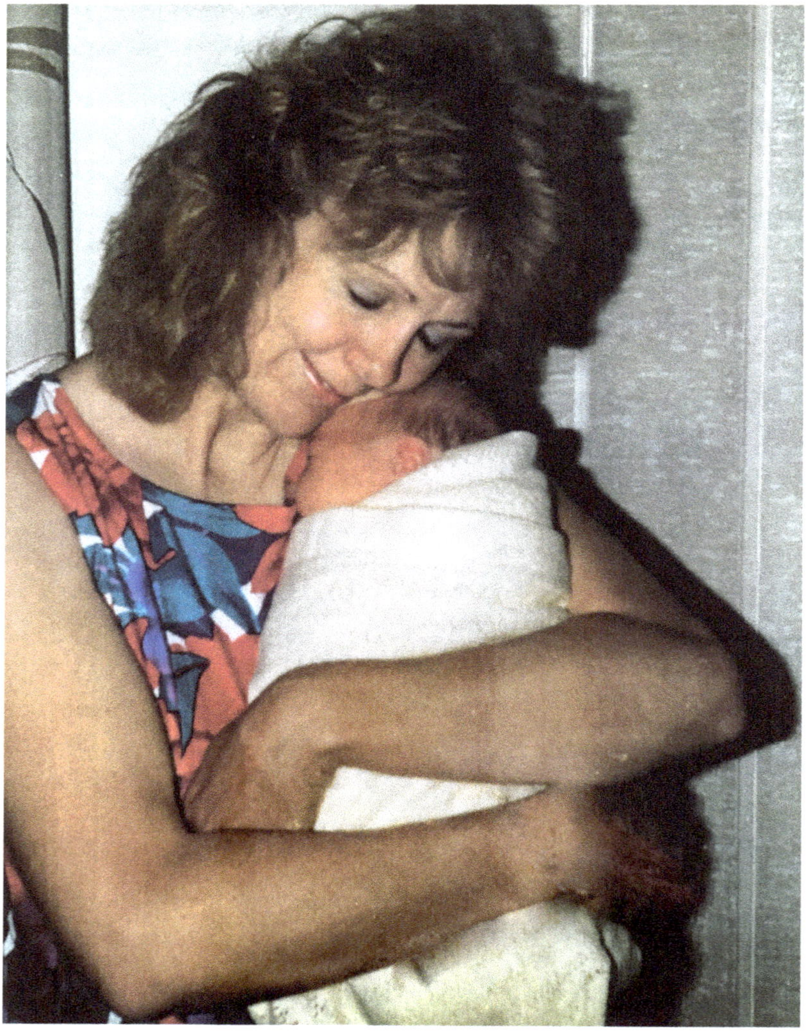

A Poem From a Mother to Her Baby

Here upon my eyes, I see your tiny body nestled in my arms.
I hadn't realised what love had really meant until I gazed
    upon you.
You are small, you are helpless, you need me so much.
What an honour it is to meet those needs and here is my
    promise to you.
I won't let you lie there to cry it out, I will pick you up and
    comfort you.
Understand that I know your cry is your communication,
    you are tired, you are hungry, you are uncomfortable.
Know that you will feel safe in your world.
Never alone, never feeling abandoned.
I am grateful that you have come into my life and know that
    I love you.

Julie Jarrett

Becoming a Parent

Becoming a Parent: A Changing Role for You and Your Partner

This is an important topic to consider as it is often not thought of prior to bringing a baby into this world.

Some thought and preparation will help put you in a better place on your journey to nurturing your baby and becoming a parent.

For the Woman

In our current times, many women in our western culture have probably had a career for a period of time and have waited until an older age before starting a family. The average age for a woman having her first baby in Australia is currently around 31 years old, compared to 22 years old in 1963.

With our separated suburban model of living, women don't often have the opportunity to observe other families nurturing their children; something that would have happened if she had lived in a community living model, as seen in many traditional societies.

There is a lot of information available for women, however they may not access this until after the baby arrives. This information can also be overwhelming, often providing contradictory points of view.

The only experiences of parenting may have been what she went through in her own childhood. An experience that may vary from wonderful to traumatic.

Due to living interstate, overseas or in full time work, extended family members may not be readily available to help, give advice, or support, creating some additional pressures.

Becoming a mother is the most amazing experience of your life. It is something that cannot be explained fully, until it happens. The value of family, friends, and building community around you, will contribute to having a more valuable and positive experience.

Preparation and understanding will also create more confidence in you as a parent.

Preparation and Ideas for Parenting

Here are some ideas for consideration when thinking about becoming a parent or before your baby arrives:

∞ Discuss with your partner what your ideal parenting styles may be and give each other a chance to be heard. If there are major differences that you feel are too difficult to come into harmony with, you may need to consider some professional guidance. It is far better to sort through this before your baby has arrived rather than after.

∞ Do the exercise at the end of this chapter – *Are we on the same page?*

- Read and access further information about parenting. I have given you some of my favourite resources at the end of this book.
- Develop a social network before the baby arrives, so it is in place for you to call upon when you need physical help, reliable advice and support, or just the company of others. Don't be afraid to ask for help; it is not a sign of weakness. People in your network will be understanding and only too willing to help. One of the hardest parts of parenting, especially in the early months, can be the feeling of loneliness and isolation.

For the Man

I can only write on this subject from my observations, what I have read, and from having discussions on this subject with men. As with women, the challenges for men when they become a parent, can be vast and overwhelming at times.

While a woman is pregnant and or birthing her child, a man most likely feels like an observer. When the baby arrives, his role changes to a participatory one.

In my observations of men who have been with their partners while they were pregnant, birthing, or in the early days of their baby's life; the majority of new fathers have shown that they are loving, protective and supportive in their new role.

In general terms, I feel some of the challenges around men at this time of their lives as a new parent, are that society has a stereotypical view of what a man's behavior should be; for example, being the breadwinner and a strong support in the background.

When I was growing up, a woman's role was seen mainly as a domestic one, caring for children and a household, with limited opportunities to do anything else. In a very short period this changed for women in the western world. They have choices available to them in education, career, family, and travel. However, the changing roles for men have not been as rapid as for women.

The strong societal and family belief systems have been embedded into their psyche, supported by the media and advertising. Through those vital years between conception and six years of age (and beyond), a male is encouraged to be seen as physically strong and more emotionally shutdown (for example, being discouraged to cry). Men are often encouraged to be more career and money driven and not to share their emotions or talk about how they feel.

It must be very difficult for men to break free from some of these stereotypes and to be their authentic selves.

Women will often seek out other women for emotional support. Programmes and events that may create change or assist you to view your life in a different way are often geared more towards women and attended more by women. Programmes and support networks are not always an available option for men, due to availability and social stigma. This can leave the male trapped in the cycle of making ends meet, building a career and losing themselves in their work, rather than focusing on development or change within themselves, or prioritising their family life.

As a society we need to recognise and support men in these changing times and understand the challenges they may face.

Giving them opportunities and support to assist in finding the authentic version of themselves; to choose the life they want.

With men and women discovering the wealth of being their authentic selves, it will allow them to be more emotionally and physically present for their family.

I asked my friend, Phil, about his experience of becoming a father. He now has 3 amazing children and was happy to share his story with me.

Becoming a Father: Phil

What was it like for you as a man becoming a father for the first time?

When we finally got to hold our baby boy after some complications, it was like that was all he needed. It was strange that his vital levels rapidly improved. I guess he just needed his mum and dad. When I was holding him for the first time, I felt this overwhelming love I can't explain or put into words. It was a feeling you just know. I remember saying to myself I would lay my life down for you, a bond that can't be explained, only felt.

How did it affect you as a man and could you talk to anyone about how you were feeling?

Once we were home and the hype had calmed down, the thoughts of how I was going to be the best dad started to have an effect on me. Not being aware of the pressure I was putting on myself, I was starting to develop an underlying stress that I was not going to be good enough for the job. This was strange because I was actually quite confident within myself. If I look back now, I will say a lot of that came from the fear of not wanting to mess things up, and from spending time listening to other parents and trying to fit it to their idea of parenthood. Today, I would suggest doing it your way. Take the advice and help where you can, but at the end of the day, make it your experience.

What challenges did you face (financially, emotionally) as a man?

We did struggle financially for a while. It did start to get a bit stressful. In my mind, I was the provider for the family, and it seemed I wasn't doing a very good job. I wasn't a big talker when it came to those thoughts and feelings, as I didn't want others to think bad of me.

How did becoming a father affect your relationship with your partner?

For me, I found it brought me and my partner closer. I walked out of the room after the complications during the birth with a complete newfound respect for my wife (and women for that matter). Later down the track our son was not sleeping well. After about a year of the late nights it started to get stressful for both of us; it was starting to become a strain on our relationship. We were both so tired. Plus, we were not getting the time together like we used to. Not going out as much, watching what we were spending, etc. We would get through it, although it did take a little adjusting, which came with its challenges, but gained us so many rewards at the same time.

Did you have sufficient support from your family and friends?

We were very lucky to have support from my wife's family, as all my family are in New Zealand. She was very close with her family, so they jumped in and helped out where they could.

How was your relationship with your baby, especially in the first months?

The first months with my boy were surreal. I would find myself just standing there now and then staring at him, asking if he was actually here. It was a strange exchange. I'll be teaching him stuff, and in turn, I found on some level he was teaching me. It was definitely a turning point in my life.

Any other information that you could provide to help fathers in the future?

To future fathers, I'm not going to lie to you, it does get challenging and will test you and your partner. What I can share with you is simply communicate and own what you're saying. What I mean by that is make the time to sit with each other now and then and voice where you are at. If you're feeling shitty about something, bring it up in a non-destructive way, but don't push it down to explode later. If you're confused or feel things are getting a bit much, just openly talk about it and express what's going on. And don't hide those tears. It is ok to cry. When something is rolling around in the mind, get it down on paper first if you feel you can't express it, then discuss it with a clear mind.

Now and then, check in with each other as individuals not as Mum, Dad, friend, etc, but where you're at as 'you'. It can be easy to get swept up as parents and do everything together which is great, but you are still your own being, also growing. Reflect on that, make a goal, and support each other to achieve it. If you can, make the start of thinking about what the best version of you looks like, put it into practice, then simply keep showing up.

The rest will take care of itself. Don't be too hard on yourself, we learn things as we go. Don't sweat the small stuff!

It is truly a gift to be a father because it can remind you that you are a part of the miracle.

Are We on the Same Page? An Exercise for You and Your Partner

Have a conversation, as a couple, to see if you have the same level of commitment and agreement regarding how you are going to nurture and parent your child.

It's about not being worried that these discussions will change your relationship, but knowing they will enhance it. A conversation can ensure that you are on a similar page when it comes to parenting and to find compromises when your opinions differ.

It is important to get your thoughts and agreements made early, preferably before you choose to have your baby. Different ideas, or parenting differences, can play a huge factor in the harmony of family life.

You may like to do this exercise at different stages of your journey. Consider seeking professional assistance if you are unable to come to acceptable compromises.

How will you look after each other's needs once your baby is born? Do you know what those needs are?

_____
_____
_____
_____
_____
_____

What are the positive and negative aspects of your childhood that you feel may affect your parenting style?

_____
_____
_____
_____
_____
_____

What uncertainties do you have with having a baby and with parenting?

_____
_____
_____
_____
_____
_____

What are the implications for you being on one wage for a period of time? What other aspects of your finances do you need to consider?

_____
_____
_____
_____
_____
_____

What lifestyle factors are important to you?

_____
_____
_____
_____

What night will be your regular date night?

_____
_____
_____
_____
_____
_____

Do you think you will need extra support to assist you with your baby? Who would you be comfortable receiving help from?

_____
_____
_____
_____
_____
_____

Do you have trusted health care professionals, for advice if required?

_____
_____
_____
_____
_____
_____

Any other things that need to be addressed?

_____
_____
_____
_____
_____

You, Your Partner, and Your Relationship

It is important to nurture your relationship with your partner both before and after you become parents. This may take forethought and effort on your part, but the rewards will be enormous for everyone in the short and long term. The stronger your relationship, the easier it will be to transition to parenthood.

Having prior knowledge, that the first few months with a new baby can sometimes feel intense and overwhelming, with little energy left for each other, is important. This will seem even harder if your relationship is not strong.

TIPS

 Making an effort within your day to spend some time together is important, before and after your baby is born.

 Go for a walk in the fresh air. It's amazing how good this will make you feel. After your baby arrives, they will be happy to snuggle up in a baby carrier. This is a good time to touch base, talk and keep the connection with each other. In the evening, when dinner has been eaten and your new baby has drifted off to sleep, avoid the temptation to switch on the TV or social media. Use this time instead to communicate with each other, even if it is only for a short time.

As you develop a relationship with your baby and understand them, things will be easier. You will gain more skills and confidence, so that things like feeding and settling your baby will take a lot less time.

 If you feel comfortable, a grandparent or carer can look after your baby for a few hours while you go out for a meal or a picnic together. Time it so that you have finished feeding your baby prior to going out. Choose a venue close by so that if your baby becomes unsettled or hungry again, a quick phone call by your carer allows you to return home quickly enough.

 If you're in a situation where you have family living interstate or overseas, there may be minimal support available for when your baby arrives, so consider asking trusted friends if they could be available to help and support you if needed. Even if you have a supportive partner, this time maybe very tiring for you both and a little extra help will be invaluable. Organise this before your baby is here and don't be afraid to ask, as most people want to help out. All babies are different, and some babies settle into early life easily whilst others don't.

If the above option is not available for you, you may wish to consider employing a postnatal (postpartum) doula to attend to you immediately following the birth and beyond. Develop a relationship with this person well before the baby arrives. A support person is not there to take over your mothering role but to support, encourage, and give you confidence.

 If you have a trusted carer, they may be happy to provide this time for you on a regular basis. Having short periods away together from your baby will ensure that you and your partner are rewarded with a healthy relationship. This is a great opportunity to communicate with each other.

 If you are isolated from family or are having to be more careful around money, create an evening at home where you eat together at the table. Create a romantic atmosphere. Make sure phones are placed away and any other distractions are off. Enjoy each other's company.

It's easy to lose that connection along the way, however, if you make a conscious effort to value your relationship on a daily basis you will reap the rewards in the long term, and this can only be a good thing for your baby and family.

You, Your Partner – Financial and Other Considerations

Financial challenges can occur, as many women go from being extremely independent and providing the household with an income, to being supported and finding it difficult to ask their partner for money. I personally found this to be incredibly challenging. I solved this situation by having a conversation with my husband and ensuring the main wage went into a joint account, with me having access to this. I also saved an amount of money that was kept in my own account. I was able to use this for any extra personal items or outings, resulting in me never feeling restricted. For this to work, there needs to be a great awareness of money. Once you go down to one wage you need to plan ahead. Maybe create a spreadsheet to work out how much money you need for the weekly or monthly bills, as well as a general budget. Conversations regarding financial changes are extremely valuable. Setting yourself up to be as financially comfortable as possible will reduce the stress in the long term.

TIPS

 Ensure you understand your financial commitments prior to having your baby so you know you are able to live without a wage, or on one wage.

 Work out with your partner if they can work closer to home, at home, or change their hours of work so they will be more available. Asking for help should not be seen as a sign of weakness.

 Understand your parental leave entitlements with your employer and the government minimum standards for support. This can assist not only financially but also help you consider options around if and when you return to work. For example, in Australia, eligible working parents receive 18 weeks of pay at the national minimum wage and are entitled to at least 12 months of unpaid leave. You need to be with the employer for at least 12 months for this to happen.

Consider the cost that is associated with having a baby. There will be several extra expenses such as purchasing baby products. Depending on the choices you make around the birth, work out the costs associated with this, e.g., midwifery, childbirth courses, doulas, doctors, hospitals, insurance costs, etc.

 Work with a trusted financial advisor if you have difficulties around financial issues. There are free services available to assist you with this if needed. Work together to decide if some of the luxuries that you can easily afford now could be forfeited for the time being. Consider things such as paid subscriptions, ordering take-away, and dining out regularly. There are easy and cheaper ways of living, such as making your lunches for the week, weekly grocery shopping instead of daily, or choosing to buy from your local farmers' market.

The cost of a daily takeaway coffee can be quite a large expenditure that you may be able to go without. Working through this well before your baby is born will relieve financial struggles later.

Perhaps start up a savings account early in your pregnancy and contribute regularly. This can be used later for such things as excursions, school fees, holidays, etc.

The environment where you live is important on a number of levels. As well as family not being available, we are living in private suburban homes where city planning has created the feeling of isolation. In more traditional village societies, family help is around for a long time after the baby has arrived. This is often missing in our more modern society and can make a big difference to the experience of having a baby. Isolation for the new mother can become an issue if not addressed prior to birth.

TIPS

 Discuss with your family how they may be able to help you after your baby is born.

 Approach community centres in your area to see what support is available. Sometimes, casual childcare will be offered as well as classes and things to do around interests you may have.

 New mothers groups provide a great level of support, friendship, and socialising for you and your new baby.

 Social media can provide information for meet up groups within your community. Many support groups are on socials and are open to asking questions, finding places to go, and things to do.

 Make sure the home you live in is in the right area for your new up and coming circumstances. Is it a long commute for your partner? Is it close to public transport if you only have one car?

These are things that you can consider prior to your baby being born.

The Practical Stuff

THIS CHAPTER COVERS everything from what equipment you may need for the newborn baby, environmental considerations, understanding health and wellness in babies, useful gift ideas from family and friends, and practical support ideas for you in the early weeks.

A List of Essentials for Your Baby

- ∞ All-in-one cotton outfits with zippers (8–10).
- ∞ Cotton singlets (8–10).
- ∞ Cloth nappies (15–20 if you wash every day or 20–30 if you plan to wash every second day) and/or disposable nappies.
- ∞ Nappy change mat.
- ∞ Cotton wool (preferably organic)/baby-friendly wipes for cleaning baby's bottom.
- ∞ Portable change mat for outings.
- ∞ Bibs (5–10).
- ∞ Night outfits (consider a sleeping bag which can keep your baby warm without blankets). Some brands will transition from an outfit that creates a swaddle effect for the newborn

baby, into a hands-free outfit, suitable for a baby who has developed the ability to roll. Some companies will also give you a guide on the thickness of the outfits in relationship to the environmental temperature. This can be a helpful in working out a comfortable temperature for your baby.
- Products for sleeping area such as a cot or bassinet, suitable mattress, mattress protector.
- Baby blankets, cotton, or woollen, depending on whether your baby is born in the summer or winter. Synthetic blankets do not 'breathe' in the same way as the natural fabrics and may cause overheating.
- A gentle natural soap suitable for babies.
- A moisturising cream with some skin barrier properties (application of the cream is only required if your baby's bottom becomes red and for keeping the skin in good condition). Consider a calendula or zinc-based cream from a health food shop or pharmacy.
- A baby sling /carrier can be extremely useful.
- A baby thermometer (see the information below on how and when to take a baby's temperature).
- Somewhere to bath your baby, whether this is a baby bath or suitable sink area.

For more information on products and safety for you baby, follow the link: www.productssafety.gov.au.

Nappy Changing

The other item that was in the drawer was the baby wipes. Many brands of wipes contain chemicals that may not be appropriate to come into the skin of a newborn baby. The skin is the largest organ of the body and things that are put on our baby's skin are absorbed quickly into their bodies.

For example, one very well-known brand of baby wipes contains ingredients such as phenoxyethanol and cocamidopropyl betaine. These chemicals have potentially dangerous by-products known to cause skin reactions and allergies. A 2014 study published in *Pediatrics* conducted by Connecticut School of Medicine found that baby wipes were responsible for a variety of itchy, scaly rashes in babies. It can also worsen pre-existing skin problems in infants and children of all ages, including but not limited to eczema, impetigo, and psoriasis.

There are some brands of wipes that contain only water and a gently natural preservative. Choose a product that easily break down (biodegradable) when disposed of.

When you are in your home it is easy to use cotton wool balls with water. Choose 100% cotton wool as some products contain synthetic fibres which don't break down easily when they are disposed of. Large amounts of pesticides are used in cotton growing, so choosing organically grown cotton wool is preferable for your baby.

Choosing a nappy can be challenging as there are many options available to purchase. A newborn baby can go through 8–12 nappies a day. For many, the choice might stop at what brand of disposable nappy is the best, however, consider using cloth nappies instead, or in conjunction with disposables can be a better choice.

Cloth nappies have evolved into a comfortable and colourful product unlike cloth nappies of old which were bulky and inefficient.

Cloth nappies hanging to dry in the sun

The advantages for using cloth nappies are:
- Better for the environment when you consider the impact disposable nappies have in landfill. They take anywhere from 250 to 500 years to break down. When faecal matter is disposed of in landfill this can contribute to contamination of the waterways.
- The initial purchase cost of cloth nappies is higher; however, as they are reused over and over again, as well as used by any other babies that come along in the future, they work out cheaper over time.

∞ Disposable nappies contain chemical products such as dyes, perfumed fragrances, and chlorines which are a concern for the health of a baby.

If you decide to use cloth nappies, ask around friends and family and look at product reviews before deciding on the best brands to purchase. You may be concerned that they will be difficult to care for, however, with modern washing machines, most of the work is done for you. A dry bucket system is used where the nappies and liners are placed after use. Laundering of the nappies can be done every alternate day if possible. It is worth purchasing a large quantity of nappies at the beginning so that you don't run out.

Bathing Tips

A bath thermometer is not necessary as it is easy enough to work out the right temperature of your baby's bath water. Immerse your arm into the water up towards your elbow. Now mix the water with this arm. When it has been well stirred, immerse your opposite arm into the water and feel it. The water temperature should feel comfortable, not too hot or cold. A temperature that you would be happy to keep your arm in, because it feels nice and comforting. Using your arms instead of your hands to test the water temperature is more accurate, as the skin on your hands may not be as sensitive as that of your arms.

Try this out before your baby even arrives so that you are confident in finding an ideal temperature before the first bath.

When it comes to the first bath for your baby, enjoy the moment. Give your baby a small feed first so she won't be focusing on an empty stomach. Have a nice warm room available as a baby generally does not like the feeling of cold air on the skin. See the picture below to see how to securely pick up your baby to be placed in the bath. Slowly immerse the lower part of her body into the water so that she has a chance to feel it. Her chest area may be above the water so use a face cloth to cover the chest then splash water over the cloth. Only keep her in the water for a short time when she is young.

Baby Soaps and Shampoos

Most baths need only to be done in plain water with no soap in it, as a baby's skin contains natural oils that are protective. Washing them off with lots of soap products is going to remove these oils.

Babies have a thinner outer layer of skin than adults. This means their skin is more sensitive to soaps and detergents. Use your judgement to decide whether to use a little soap when washing your baby's hair or bottom area. There are many brands and products available on the market. I encourage you to read the labels carefully, understand what the ingredients are, and purchase products without harmful ingredients in them which could include sodium lauryl sulphate, alcohol, parabens and colourants.

Depending on your baby, you may only need to bath your baby every few days, unless you are using the bathing for settling and relaxation in the evenings.

Prams

A baby carrier will often be more than sufficient for carrying your baby around in the early part of her life as it keeps her close to you. If you carry your baby regularly you will gain more and more strength in your body, enabling you to easily carry your baby as she grows. A pram may be useful as your baby gets older, or if walking longer distances, or if you are experiencing physical strain from carrying your baby.

When you decide on a pram, the things that you need to consider are:
∞ The cost.
∞ The ease of folding and putting it in and out of a vehicle.
∞ Covers that are removable and washable.
∞ The weight of the pram.
∞ Storage on the pram for nappy bags, drink bottle, phone etc.
∞ Practicality if you decide to have another baby.

Ideally the pram manufacturer would make it a requirement to supply their products with easily removable, washable covers on all their prams. It is not the pram structure that wears out, it is the covers which become stained. If the covers are unable to be removed to be washed or replaced, the whole pram is often abandoned and ends up in landfill.

Baby Car Seats

As many of us often travel numerous kilometers in our vehicles, it is important to ensure your baby is safe and comfortable in a car seat.

Things to consider:
- Compliance with your country's safety standards. In Australia and New Zealand, a standards sticker is included on these products: AS/NZS 1754.
- Different car seats are required for the different ages/sizes of your child.
- The car seat needs to be correctly fitted into the car.

If buying a secondhand car seat, do so with caution as you would need to know that it meets safety standards. Consider the history of the seat, such as whether it's been involved in any accidents, the condition, and whether all the parts, straps and instruction book are included.

Thermometers and Fevers

A digital thermometer is an appropriate gift. It is ideal for taking a baby's temperature and is important to have. The knowledge and understanding about how to take a baby's temperature correctly is also important for parents. I believe this is something that all new parents should be taught. When your baby has arrived, practice taking the temperature when your baby is well. This will give you confidence that the temperature is accurate, if the baby is unwell.

Fevers have always been seen as something that needs to be reduced or eliminated; however, we need to understand why a fever is present.

"Fever (a high temperature) is common in children. Fever is a normal response to many illnesses, the most common being an infection in the body. Fever itself is usually not harmful. In fact, it helps the body's immune system fight off infection. While fevers can be concerning for parents, doctors will usually be more concerned about what is causing the fever, not what the child's temperature is. It is more important for you to monitor any symptoms of the underlying illness, rather than the fever itself." Refer to www.rch.org.au/kidsinfo_sheets/Fever_in_children

So, you may see fever differently now. A fever can be a friend in this situation. It is a good idea to download a fact sheet such as the one above and keep it handy. This will help you determine what to do if your baby is unwell. It will help you to decide whether to keep the baby well hydrated and cared for at home or to seek medical attention.

A baby's normal temperature is generally between 36.4 and 37.4 degrees. If a baby is under three months of age and has a fever above 38 degrees, even if they have no other symptoms, take them to be assessed by a doctor.

TIP

When a baby is unwell and can be managed at home it is helpful to have some safe and effective home remedies to help

> your baby feel more comfortable. Homeopathic remedies are one safe option. A trained practitioner who can give you the appropriate remedy and dosage for infants is recommended.

Aromatherapy oils can also be effective; however, as babies are small and sensitive, only some oils are suitable for them. Choose the oils from a reputable company that produce a high-quality product. Fragrance oils are man-made synthetic oils and are not the same as aromatherapy oils which are plant-based oils. For the correct usage of aromatherapy oils consult an Aromatherapist. A useful book to have on hand is *The Fragrant Pharmacy* written by Valerie Ann Worwood.

Gifts to Give or Receive for a New Baby

STORY

My friend is having a baby, what will I give her?

I remember visiting a relative once and being shown the new nursery, freshly painted, and decorated, and beautifully presented.

We went over to the chest of drawers that were filled with gifts from well-meaning friends. I was taken aback by some of the products I saw. Plenty of different brands of chemical wipes, as well as lots of different brands of painkillers and other medicines.

If a baby is unwell and requires medication, these should be obtained at the time and be specific for the illness. The medications that were sitting in the draw may never be

> used and then would need to be disposed of correctly as the medication reached or went beyond its expiry date.
>
> These would not have been my choice of gifts to give for a baby. Many of these gifts are given at baby showers and are not always beneficial.

Baby Gifts

If your friend is having a baby, here are some useful gift ideas:

- ∞ Consider purchasing an outfit for the baby for when he/she is older, for example 6–12 months old. The mother may have already obtained outfits for the newborn period and be gifted newborn sized clothing. They grow out of them quickly and the larger clothing will be appreciated as they get older.
- ∞ Get together with a group of friends and contribute towards an empowering childbirth course. Check with your friend first that this is something that they would like to do. It may have been something that your friend had heard about, or had wanted to do, but was unable to afford. The knowledge, confidence and support that a woman and her partner receive through a quality course is invaluable. I am biased towards the courses that I have taught to many couples as a Hypnobirthing Australia practitioner. I have seen how confident the couples become after completing the course, and from the follow up they give me after they have birthed their baby. There are other courses available too, so it's important to find one that suits the mother's needs.
- ∞ Cloth nappies are a great gift idea. They can be an expensive item to initially purchase, however, in the longer term

(especially if another child is planned in the future) they save money and are more environmentally friendly.
- A massage voucher. Having a baby and the weeks following can be physically and mentally challenging for many women. To have some moments to feel valued and pampered, as well as having a masseur working on any areas of stress or strain in the physical body, would be appreciated.
- A beautiful, handcrafted wool blanket is a great gift and one that the baby will use for many years to come.
- A chew toy to assist the baby when teething.
- A financial gift for the baby's future.

Other Practical Helpful Ideas

Looking at the bigger picture and educating ourselves of what we do on a daily basis helps us in making considered choices to create the healthy world that we want our children to live in. Here are some practical ideas:
- Before you have your baby, and if you have a freezer available, prepare and freeze healthy meals. These will be invaluable in the early weeks if you feel too tired to prepare food. Pull the meal out of the freezer in the morning to defrost and then there is little to do at the end of the day. It is food that you have prepared, so it is unlikely to have any upsetting effects on your baby (through breastmilk).
- Have a storage container in the boot of your car filled with extra nappies, cotton wool balls, face washers, water in a sealed container, baby outfits (at least two), blankets, cotton breast shields, extra outfit for yourself, and some empty containers

for any soiled items. You then only need to carry the basics items for immediate use, in a small backpack (therefore hands free) when you go out.

∞ If your family is available to help out after the birth, but you believe their ideas are outdated, you could consider offering them a course to update their knowledge. For example, if it is the grandparents that will be available for you, they may benefit from a course such as grandparent's classes. These are available privately or through maternity hospitals.

∞ Be mindful when burning candles within your home, as some candles have synthetic fragrances which could trigger allergies and be detrimental to the health of your baby.

∞ Learn about, and use natural products for cleaning the house before and after your baby's arrival. Chemical-laden products are not good for our health and babies are very sensitive to these products. There are many easy to source products that are effective cleaners.

Natural Cleaning Product Recipes

∞ ⅓ cup of white vinegar to ⅔ cup of water makes a good general-purpose cleaner.

∞ 3 parts baking soda to 1 part water is good for cleaning more stubborn stained areas. Add a drop of eucalyptus or lemon grass essential oil to create a pleasant and clean smell.

The Health and Vitality of the New Mother

THINK OF YOUR body as an amazing machine that has been developed and adapted over thousands and thousands of years. It is so specialised, and when it is maintained with the highest quality care, this machine works with precision, smoothness, and is a joy to behold.

If we place substances that are substandard into that machine, or care for it infrequently, then it will not perform at its optimum level. It rattles, splutters, and it is noisy. We know that the human body is not a mechanical machine, however, this is a good analogy. If we feed ourselves with appropriate portions of clean, fresh, pesticide free and enzyme rich foods, our human bodies will reflect the good care we are taking of it. If we feed ourselves with sugary, highly processed and/or fat laden foods, in a toxic environment, you will have a body that functions in a substandard way. It is a concept that is simple and easy. So, how do we achieve this?

Setting yourself up for success means making a conscious effort to clean up your lifestyle, preferably before you even have your baby. Doing this before or while you are pregnant is an ideal time, but it is never too late. The body is amazing and can repair itself very quickly if it is given the right conditions.

Making life easier with regards to food and food preparation is a good place to start.

The Kitchen

Your pantry should be kept relatively empty of foods that are full of additives and preservatives (used to help increase shelf life). Additives and preservatives are not the best things to be placing into our bodies as they cause lethargy, weight gain, heart problems and many other related health issues. Many processed foods also contain unwanted sugars and unhealthy fats.

Have food that is fresh and rich in enzymes in your fridge, on your kitchen bench, and in your window or vegetable garden.

Enzymes

A discussion about good health would not be complete without learning something about the importance of enzymes.

Enzymes are vital to assist the food breaking down in our system, before entering the blood. For every chemical reaction in our body, enzymes are working to build and maintain our body, our life force.

Our bodies may be flooded with items for health such as vitamins, minerals, and proteins but without adequate enzyme activity, our health begins to suffer.

Enzymes occur naturally in our bodies; however, they exist in limited supply. They are also present in our food, but they are easily reduced or destroyed by processing and heat.

With an intake of food that has reduced, or is devoid of enzyme activity, the body must now use its enzyme resources to digest food. This consequently takes the enzymes away from their important role of running and maintaining important body systems such as the brain, heart, kidneys, and muscles, setting ourselves up over the long term for ill health.

How to get more enzyme activity from our food:

∞ Eating an abundance of food in its raw state where possible.
∞ Eating food that is ripening, as this is when enzyme activity is at its best.

Enzyme inhibitors are present in foods such as raw nuts and seeds, as well as some in peas, beans, and lentils. Cooking destroys the inhibitors as well as the enzymes; however, sprouting foods, when appropriate, will maintain the enzymes. To sprout food, choose beans or legumes such as mung beans or alphalfa, then soak them in water in a container that can be rinsed and drained twice a day. Before you know it, you will have nutritional sprouts for your salads.

Foods such as bananas, avocados and mangoes are a particularly good source of enzymes. A baby receives an abundance of enzymes from the mother's breastmilk.

Keeping your pantry relatively empty and your fridge and kitchen bench full of fresh produce does require planning and organisation, but your body and mind will function so much better for doing this. Follow these easy steps:

1. Let's sort out the pantry. Leave a few basic things like tomato paste, rice, and tomato sauces. Find products that are preferably free from sugar and unhealthy oils (canola oil). Try to use products with glass jars, as this will avoid contamination from plastic and tin containers.
2. Start a sprouting shelf. Gather some sprouting containers. You can buy them online or from your local health food shop. Sprout things such as alfalfa or mung beans. They are great additives to your salads and rich in enzymes.
3. Purchase as much of your fresh fruit and vegetables as organically grown, or as pesticide free as possible.
4. Start a vegetable patch. This does not have to be large. No matter what size accommodation you live in, you can still have a vegetable garden, even if it is in pots on the veranda or patio. Lettuce and herbs, including parsley and coriander, are great for a small garden. You can pick leaves off these plants as you need them.

Food Preparation Made Easy

If you are busy, choose a day where you prepare a variety of meals for the week. This is great fun to do with a friend! These meals can be kept in the fridge for a few days, or frozen. Use these main meals each day and simply add fresh salads, lightly steamed or raw vegetables (hopefully some from your own garden).

As well as preparing your main meals, you can also prepare a large salad. If you leave out the ingredients that are on the moist side like tomatoes and avocado and put them in just prior to eating, this salad can last a couple of days in the fridge. A sheet of paper towel placed in the base of the bowl of salad will also help to keep it fresh.

After you go shopping, place your fresh produce into a container in the fridge with paper towel on the bottom and the lid on to maintain freshness. If you keep all your salad items in the one container it is easy for preparation.

Salad Item Shopping List Example

Carrots	Tomatoes	Celery
Cucumbers	Radishes	Apple
Avocado	Cabbage	Rocket
Lettuce	Spinach	Shallots

Homemade Dressing

This makes a delicious, easy dressing. Combine all ingredients together and drizzle on your salad just prior to serving:

Mustard	Garlic
Balsamic Vinegar	Natural Honey
Olive Oil	

Fruit

In recent times, fruit has been regarded as negative due to the high levels of sugar. People perceive that fruit has too much sugar and have been avoiding it altogether. However, fruit contains fructose (a form of sugar) which is different to the processed, cane sugars. Fruit is safe to eat. It is healthy and necessary for our well-being. The best way to eat fruit is on its own, as it digests better than being eaten on top of a heavy meal.

Healthy Snack Ideas

Motherhood is a remarkably busy time in your life and the temptation to go to the pantry and get a sweet biscuit because you are hungry can be all too easy. Here are some remarkably simple and tasty snack ideas, and you will feel so much better if you have these readily available. You will be able to care for your baby and your family much better, as you will experience more energy and wellbeing.

∞ Avocado and tomato on rice crackers.
∞ Carrot sticks and hummus.
∞ Nuts such as walnuts, almonds, Brazil nuts.
∞ Dried fruit (preferably when the season is abundant – with your own food dehydrator).

This list is endless. Be creative and make your snacks tasty and enjoyable.

Water

The water that we drink needs to be in its purest form for the health of our bodies. Water often contains added chlorine (for water disinfecting) and fluoride. These substances can be harmful to our health. The simplest way to remove chlorine is to let it evaporate from the water.

Water filters remove harmful additives from your water, such as chlorine, pesticides, metals, and other chemicals such as fluoride, which may not be beneficial for your health. Make sure you do your research to ensure that you find the appropriate filter that is right for you.

There are some guidelines about how much water you should drink each day, however, it is hard for anyone to give you the exact amount you require, because we are all built so differently. For example, a small built woman would require a lot less water than a large framed man. Or, you might live in a cold climate and require less water than someone who lives in a hot climate. Someone who does a lot of exercise will need more water than someone who is not so active.

How to work out the quantity of water you may require:

1. Thirst can be the latter sign of dehydration, so try and ensure you don't get to the thirsty stage.
2. You can be guided by what your urine looks like. If you have not drunk enough water, your urine will be darker yellow in colour.
3. Drink most of your water between meals. Large amounts of water at mealtimes will reduce the effectiveness of the gastric digestive juices.
4. Have a water bottle near you during the day to encourage you to take sips of water. It is better to take sips of water rather than one big drink all at once.
5. Store your water for transporting in glass or stainless steel rather than plastic bottles.
6. Avoid excessive amounts of tea and coffee, as your body requires fluid to process these. Herbal teas, however, can be very beneficial. If possible, obtain these as dried leaf teas, rather than tea bags, and preferably from organic sources.

The value of water for your body

Up to 60% of the adult human body is water
70-80% of a newborn baby's body is water

The brain consists of 73% water

Water boosts your energy

The plasma in the blood is made up of 92% water

Muscles and kidneys are 79% water

Promotes healthy skin

Protects and moisturises our joints

Heart consists of 73% water

Moisturises the air in our lungs to assist with metabolism

You can see how drinking water is so important to the human body

www.motherandbaby-workinginharmony.com.au

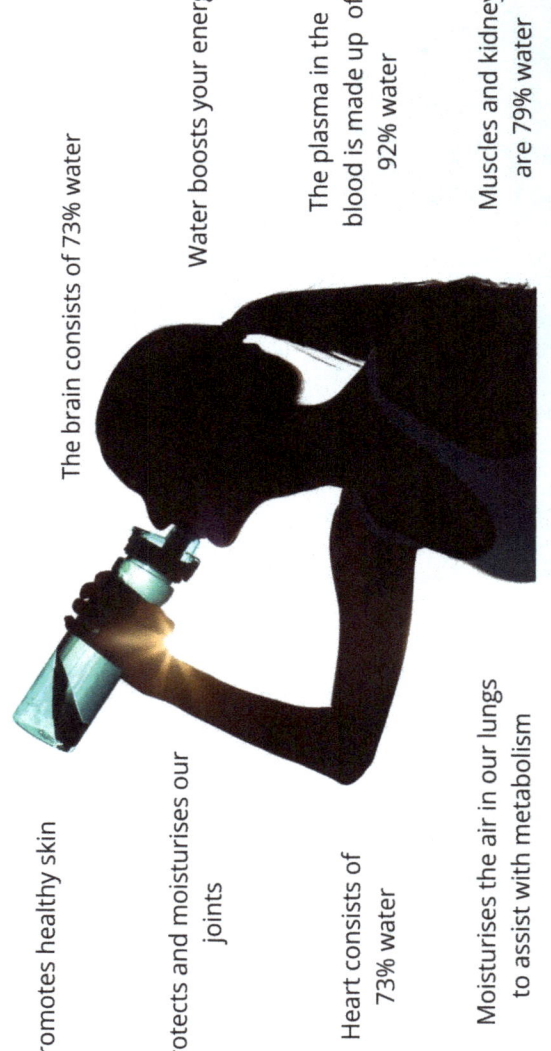

7. Consider the temperature that you drink your water. In many cultures around the world, drinking cold water is not considered beneficial for the body, or for the efficient digestion of food.
8. A slice of lemon or some mint can make water taste delicious and refreshing. Lemon also assists in detoxifying the body and mint reportedly soothes indigestion, wind, and griping problems.

I came across this information from a Japanese scientist, Dr. Masaru Emoto. He revolutionised the idea that our thoughts and intentions impact the properties of water. He was able to make crystals by freezing water and when he examined these crystals under the microscope, he noticed major differences in their structure, when exposed to different words, emotions, music, and environments.

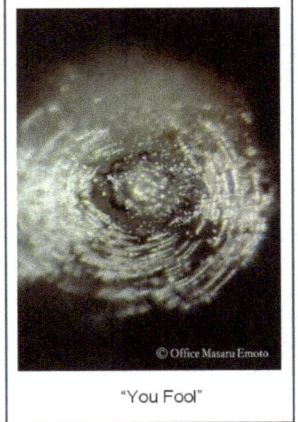

"You Fool"

"Thank You"

* Source of photos @Office Masaru Emoto
website – https://www.masaru-emoto.net/jp/message/

As our bodies are made of around 60% water, I found this interesting. What if the messages we said to ourselves really do have a positive effect on our bodies and is provable?

These photos were taken of the water molecules after they were removed from the different containers that had the words, 'You Fool' and 'Thank You' taped on the outside of them with the words facing in towards the water. The molecules were frozen and examined and a notable difference was seen.

Setting Yourself Up for Success

Eating mostly organic, fresh produce, and freshly prepared foods with small amounts of quality protein will go a long way to ensuring that you have a healthy eating lifestyle.

Once you have organised your fridge and cleaned up your pantry, the following steps will assist you in being prepared to go to work or on an outing. These ideas will reduce unnecessary stress.

TIPS

 Take your own ingredients out with you: To avoid the temptation of purchasing 'quick fix foods' (which are generally expensive and unhealthy) place your prepared food into glass containers. Place the containers into a cold storage box, with freezer blocks, to ensure that your healthy food is kept cool and available.

 Get into the habit of taking your own filtered water with you wherever you go. This will ensure you are hydrated throughout the day, and is good for the environment, as you are

> not purchasing bottled water or soft drinks in plastic bottles. Have an extra bottle of water in the car, particularly on long trips.

How we eat our food is also important. Get into the habit of sitting down at a table to eat. This allows you to be mindful of what you are eating and how it will nourish your body. Mindful eating and having gratitude for your food will assist in keeping you healthy.

Rushing food down on the run is not good for you or your body. Chew your food slowly. Have respect for how the food has been grown and harvested. Consider the hard work that has gone into providing you with this food.

Keeping your conversation at the dinner table as light as possible will enhance your experience and help your body to digest your food in a beneficial way.

Listening to Your Body

Many of our eating habits stem from our childhood; however, other messages that affect our eating come from messages received through the media. We are bombarded with subtle, and not so subtle, messages from social media, television, movies, advertisements, newspapers and magazines.

As a child, you may have had parents who insisted that you eat all the food in front of you, as they may have lived in times when food was scarce or expensive. Junk food and sweet desserts may have been used as a bargaining tool to get you to eat your vegetables. Your meal times may have been dictated by the clock, and not by when you were hungry.

These childhood messages, and events around food, can become an unconscious influence on the decisions you make around your eating habits today.

When you eat a food, begin to listen to your body and how it feels after you have consumed it. If it makes your stomach feel uncomfortable, assess to see if that is a food your body is happy to consume. Be more observant about how each food is contributing to the harmony of your body.

If you experience food cravings, check whether you have any deficiencies in what you are eating and correct those deficiencies. For example, you may be craving chocolate, perhaps indicating that you are low in magnesium. Try consuming magnesium-rich foods and see if those craving settle. Sometimes, supplements are required, as food can be deficient in vitamins and minerals if they are not grown in nutrient rich soil or stored correctly. If you feel that you require some assistance with your diet, perhaps seeking further advice from a health professional, such as a nutritionist or dietician will be beneficial.

Exercising

If you lead a sedentary lifestyle, this may create challenges for you.

A baby, on average, will weigh 3,300 grams and it takes a bit of muscle power to comfortably pick them up and support them. Consider some gentle weight training before your baby arrives, especially of the arms, hands, and shoulders. There are other gentle options such as regular walking, yoga, chi gong, or pilates, that will assist with your overall strength.

When your baby arrives, exercise does not have to be complicated. Going out into the fresh air for a walk with your new baby on a regular basis will be beneficial. Keep it simple. If you have a carrier, carry your baby close to your chest. Babies love the movement, hearing your voice, and just being next to you. Having sunshine on your skin increases your vitamin D levels, an important factor for staying healthy.

Stress

Another aspect of health is stress. Our world is becoming increasingly stressful, with so many more things to do which creates less time for you to relax, unwind and stay connected.

Pregnant women in the workforce are often under a lot of stress, while trying to manage all the other duties and responsibilities in their lives. Some communities that women live in are not safe and create an environment that is stressful and fearful. As a result, these women are constantly experiencing an excessive release of stress hormones.

Evidence produced by Dr Bruce Lipton shows that the brain of an embryo belonging to a mother under constant stress while pregnant, develops differently. The brain of a stressed embryo develops a larger area that prepares for fight or flight, while the area for nurturing, thriving, and nourishing is much smaller.

It is also important to understand that constant stress creates a brain that does not think in a rational and logical way. When our cerebral thinking brain is not being activated, it is the hindbrain which just wants to run away (fight or flight).

Stress also reduces our immunity. In a stressed situation, the immune system has a reduced ability to fight off toxins and foreign substances, leaving the body more vulnerable to disease.

The conscious mind can rewrite your genetics. This is called Epigenetics and is the study of how your behaviours and environment can cause changes that affect the way your genes work. This is powerful knowledge when used.

Think of a scale with love on one side and fear on the other, with indifference in the middle (see below). Currently, where do you think you are emotionally on that scale? How are your stress levels? Which end of the scale are you at?

If you are close to the fear end of your scale, how could you change elements of your life to be closer to the area of love and nurturing?

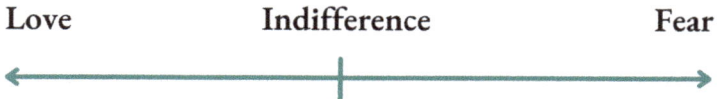

You are the genetic engineer for your child, so be conscious and aware of what happens during pregnancy and avoid stress as much as possible.

Sleep

As adults, we value our sleep; it can be a difficult adjustment to be meeting the needs of a new baby, especially at night. Adjusting your own sleep patterns can significantly help. A consistent sleep schedule is especially important for health. This can be a challenge when you have a newborn baby, however, once things have settled down you can begin to find a regular sleep time.

When your baby is needing frequent feeding, settling, and comfort during the night, take opportunities during the day to have rest times, especially in the early months of your baby's life. Not putting yourself under pressure to achieve all the household chores, or all you did before, will benefit you and your baby. Self-care is extremely important at this time.

Be mindful of the electronic devices kept in your bedroom. Computers and phones that are in the bedroom emit a blue light that can make your brain think it's daytime, delaying the release of melatonin. Melatonin helps you sleep.

If you are having trouble getting up in the morning, start by opening the curtains to let the daylight in. This will reset the circadian rhythm (sleep/wake cycle) of the brain, boosting the release of hormones that bring up your temperature and give you your energy.

Breastfeeding Your Baby

MORE THAN EVER women are now understanding the importance of breastfeeding the way nature intended. There are many different elements to breastmilk, including vitamins and minerals that contribute towards the healthy development of your baby. Specific components in breastmilk also contribute to a strong, healthy immune system.

World governing bodies recommend exclusive breastfeeding for six months. Breastfeeding with the addition of solid food is recommended from six months until two years of age or longer. The mother and baby need to be in harmony with each other when making these decisions.

96% of women want to breastfeed their baby; however, by the age of three months, only 39% of babies are being exclusively breastfed. Exclusive breastfeeding means a baby is receiving only breast milk, no other liquids, or solids. By five months of age the percentage of exclusive breastfeeding drops off rapidly to 15%.

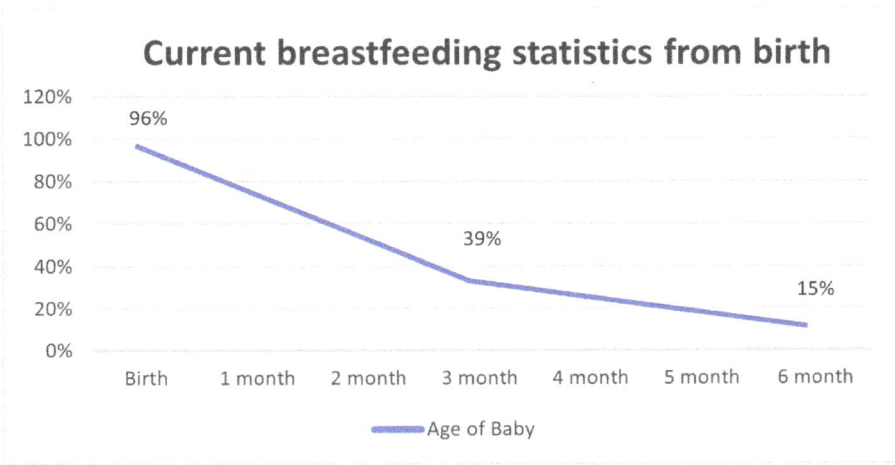

* Statistics from the *2010 Australian National Infant Feeding Survey*

Understanding Breastfeeding and Being Change Makers

If we look into the history of breastfeeding over the last two to three generations, this may help us to understand what breastfeeding looks like now and into the future.

In the early 1900's breastfeeding rates started to fall, so that by the 1950's the initiation rate was 25% and by 1972 only 22%. There were many reasons for this, from changing birth practises, centralising nurseries that cared for all babies away from their mothers, and the promotion of breastmilk substitutes by health professionals and powerful manufacturing companies.

The support from health professionals for women to successfully breastfeed their babies was also limited.

Following WWII, more women were in the workforce and working away from home. After the birth of their babies, they found minimal support from workplaces to support continued breastfeeding.

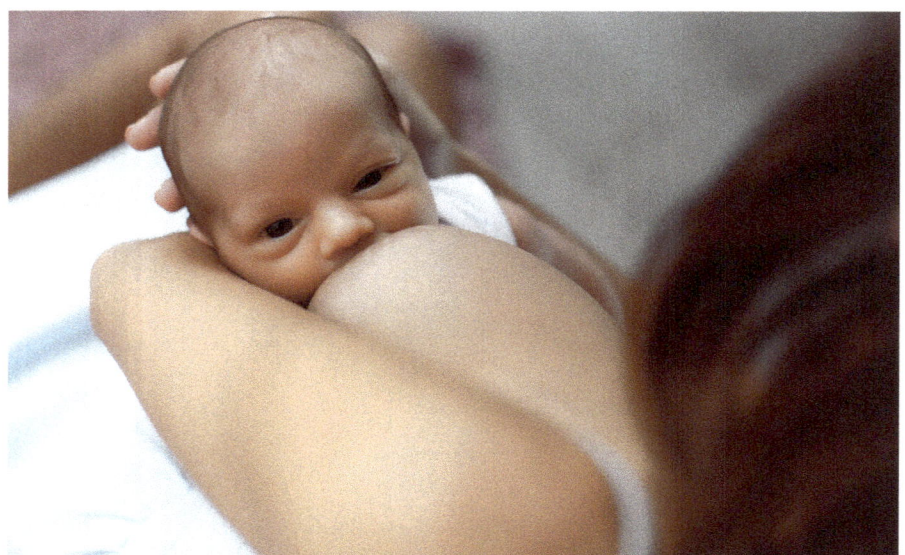

"Breastfeeding is one of the most effective ways to ensure child health and survival" –
World Health Organisation.

In the early 70's women's movement groups were becoming more common, allowing women to voice their needs more. Groups such as the Nursing Mother's Association of Australia, now known as Australian Breastfeeding Association (ABA), and world governing agencies were implementing changes. Hospitals and health professionals in these areas followed on with changes to policies and procedures to support breastfeeding.

These are some of the policies and regulations that have contributed to the evolution of breastfeeding in modern times:

- **1976 CXA 2 – 1976, Statement on Infant Feeding** – statement on the problems of infant feeding and the value of breastmilk as an ideal food for the infant in the first six months of its life.
- **Declaration of Alma Atta** – a holistic approach to primary health care.

- **1978** The first **Kangaroo Mother Care** (KMC) – continuous skin to skin contact in an upright position instigated in response to high morbidity and mortality in low-birth-weight infants in crowded, poorly resourced neonatal intensive care units.
- **1979 IBFAN** – International Baby Food Action Network to regulate marketing practices.
- **1979 CEDAW** – Convention on the Elimination of all forms of discrimination against women.
- **1983 LLLI** – Peer counselling, supporting more wider education in breastfeeding.
- **1985 ILCA** – International Lactation Consultant Association.
- **1989** Ten Steps to Successful Breastfeeding.
- **1990** Innocenti Declaration – says that all women should be enabled to practice exclusive breastfeeding and all infants should be fed exclusively on breastmilk.
- **2004 World Breastfeeding Week** – exclusive breastfeeding theme.
- **2004–2006** U.S. National Breastfeeding Awareness campaign.

I commenced my nursing and midwifery training during these times when there was limited understanding of the importance of breastfeeding.

Babies were placed in nurseries and only brought out to the mother at feed times. Timing regulated when a baby could feed, and this would generally be only every four hours. As well as this, midwives were instructing women to limit the amount of time that a baby could be on each breast. For the first 24 hours the mother was encouraged to only feed on each side for three minutes. By day four the baby could feed for 10 minutes on either side. The idea behind the time limitations was that nipples needed time to adjust to a baby being on the breast, not realising that that they could be on a breast for a long time without pain or discomfort if *they were positioned correctly*. This practice was not conducive to good breast drainage, and consequently, women were experiencing pain and very engorged breasts when their milk supply increased, around the fourth day following birth.

We now have a vast array of breastfeeding knowledge; however, the remaining beliefs from that time are continuing today. Many modern women, the older generations, and some health professionals still believe that babies understand clocks. They don't!

Babies have built in appetites like you and I, and they know when they are hungry and when they are full. That is why they need to be demand fed (unless there is a medical reason). Just like us, if you eat when you are not hungry, you either don't feel like eating much, or you overeat and then regret it later.

There is also what I call an urban myth around breastfeeding, with women believing breastfeeding is painful for several weeks before the nipples toughen up. This urban myth continues to be passed on through the generations and through families and friends.

When I have taught antenatal classes, I ask class participants what they know or have heard about breastfeeding. Inevitably, the first thing they mention is, that it is painful.

Breastfeeding should not be painful for the majority of women. The word breastfeeding means that the baby attaches to breast tissue around the nipple and not onto the nipple. Attaching onto the nipple is what contributes or causes a painful experience.

In our society, we often have outdated breastfeeding knowledge from our older generations, as most babies ended up being bottle fed in those times. Women rarely see other women breastfeeding and the breasts are either covered up or a woman removes herself to another room to feed her baby, due to societal expectations and lack of confidence.

Difficulties can arise when a woman becomes a mother and believes that breastfeeding should be natural and easy. Yes, breastfeeding is natural; however, because it is a skill that is learnt by women (instinctive for the baby), a certain amount of practice is required to master it. Like anything in life, some people pick up the skill easily and others find it more difficult.

Consider the more traditional societies that live in community settings. Children view women feeding their babies from a very young age, especially in cultures where clothing is minimal. Breasts are seen as a normal part of women.

STORY

I helped a woman who was motivated to breastfeed; however, she was experiencing painful nipples and other breastfeeding problems. She had been told this pain would last for several weeks, until the nipples became used to it (they don't). She had also experienced sensitive nipples during her pregnancy (which is common). This added to her pre-existing belief that breastfeeding would be painful.

She continued to breastfeed her baby and to tolerate the pain, not realising that the baby was not attaching properly, and that this was the issue.

Each feed became more and more painful, and the mother became reluctant to even want to put her baby back onto her breast. It was creating many follow up problems such as emotional upsets, interferences with their mother/baby connection, breast engorgement, and an episode of mastitis. It was a domino effect.

Once this mother was shown the right way to attach her baby to her breast, she experienced breastfeeding without pain for the first time. After gaining experience with the new technique, the mother looked forward to feeding her baby. She continued to have a comfortable breastfeeding experience, contributing to her baby having a wonderful start to life.

Be patient with yourself as, for most women, it will get easier, especially if you learn the correct skills from the beginning. Surround yourself with knowledgeable and supportive people.

STORY

A woman I went to see recently stated that she had large nipples and was finding it difficult to get her baby onto the breast. She felt that this baby had a smaller mouth than her first baby. It had taken her a few months to get her first baby to attach directly to the breast.

I shared with her that I had seen many women in similar situations who had managed good attachment with some guidance. I also knew that it would be much easier for her as it was her second baby, so the confidence and handling of her baby was already there.

We worked together to make sure every element of good attachment with her baby was in place. On the third attempt deep attachment was achieved and her baby happily commenced feeding with deep jaw movements, audible swallowing, and no pain. Later in the afternoon when I dropped in to visit this mother, she told me that she had fed again, and it had been successful.

It was a good lesson in belief. She was close to deciding not to continue direct breastfeeding, but to express and bottle feed her baby. She was so glad she made the decision to get further advice.

There is a lot of information available about breastfeeding. Be mindful as to the validity of your resources. There is a recommended resource chapter at the end of this book, and I have also included a link to my website which includes information and videos for visual learning.

Refer to: www.motherandbaby-workinginharmony.com.au

STORY

Another woman I remember well came to me with a two-week-old baby. She had very tender nipples and had been resting them and expressing her milk for her baby. She told me she had tender nipples even when she was not pregnant, so she wasn't surprised that she was suffering pain now.

She had a good supply of milk. I asked her what the attachment had been like when her baby was breastfeeding directly. She felt it had been fine apart from the sensitivity of her nipples.

Now having the opportunity to observe a feed, I guided her towards making some simple adjustments. Suddenly she looked up at me and said, "Actually it's not painful anymore."

Her belief that the pain she was experiencing was due to the fact that she was normally sensitive convinced her that she would need to put up with the pain.

In this story and the previous story, the beliefs of each woman (large nipples, small mouth, very sensitive nipples) had been stopping them looking for solutions earlier on.

Be kind to yourself.

The basic set up for attaching a baby on to the breast will be the same no matter what size your breasts, the shape of your nipples or the position you choose to feed your baby in. Some breast and nipple shapes are more challenging, however with the correct guidance and information this will help overcome these challenges.

As a Lactation Consultant, I work closely with women to assist them to improve their breastfeeding experience. I really believe that we can empower each woman to have the knowledge and confidence in their ability to feed their baby and to understand when their baby is thriving on their milk. I encourage the women I have worked with to share their newfound knowledge and skills with the other women in their world as they become mothers. My hope is that this will have a positive effect as the word spreads.

Finding Solutions

When a woman is pregnant it is important to be giving her correct, helpful and adequate information about breastfeeding.

If you are birthing in a hospital setting, the child birth education classes offered may incorporate a breastfeeding component, that will be beneficial for you. You can seek out classes run by breastfeeding organisations, or Lactation Consultants can also offer more comprehensive breastfeeding classes and support, following the birth of your baby.

The immediate time after a birth can be a challenging time for women to learn new skills and retain information. This can be due to a combination of factors such as hormonal changes, tiredness, stress, or medications. It is important to understand that there are a multitude of opinions and advice given when you have your baby. It is essential not to become overwhelmed. If you have any concerns, or you feel that the information is contradictory, ask questions about the information you are given.

For example, if you are advised to feed your baby every three to four hours, ask why. If the answer is understandable, e.g. the baby has lost weight or has increasing jaundice, then this maybe correct. If no good reason is given and you understand demand feeding, then decide for yourself what suits you and your baby.

Advice given may well have been appropriate at the time for a situation, however this information may be inadequate when the circumstances change. For example, a sleepy baby in the early days may need to be woken for feeds if they are not feeding well and have a low output of urine. It would be inappropriate for this same baby to continue to be woken up frequently when it was a week old, with the mother's milk fully in, the baby feeding well and the urine (and bowel) output adequate.

If you are experiencing difficulties in the immediate time after having your baby, your midwives and carers are there to assist you. Please ask for their help. Midwives can teach you the new skills you require for comfortable, pain free attachment, learning to observe when a baby is feeding well (milk transfer or comfort feeding), and when a baby is needing a feed.

A high level of support, especially in the first week(s), is very important in gaining confidence and the skills needed for long term success in breastfeeding. When insufficient support is available to women in their efforts to breastfeed, they understandably give up.

Women who have difficulties in supplying their babies with their own breast milk due to health, anatomical, hormonal, or other issues beyond their control, need extra support and understanding.

The level of support may range from that of family and friends to professional guidance.

Safe supplies of human milk for babies who are unable to be breastfed are only available through milk banks in some hospitals and currently (in Australia) it is only available for premature babies in special care nurseries.

Before the Baby Arrives

In the middle weeks of the pregnancy, the cells in the breast change into cells that are capable of milk production. You may notice breast changes and finding a comfortable well fitted bra is important. Breast changes vary for different women during pregnancy.

No special preparation is required for the nipples, however, avoid soap or shampoo in this area as it will have a drying effect.

During pregnancy, from approximately 16 weeks onwards, milk is produced in your breasts. This early milk is small in quantity and is called colostrum. Your placenta is full of hormones that stop large quantities of colostrum from being produced. Once your placenta comes away after birth, your body gets the message to start producing increased quantities of breast milk.

Expressing Colostrum

Consider doing some expressing of the colostrum from your breasts before your baby arrives. This can be done from 36 weeks onwards. It can be collected in a syringe, labelled and frozen. If for any reason in the first few days after birthing your baby, your baby does not attach to the breast, or if your baby is separated from you for medical reasons, this will be available for them.

In Australia, between the years 2011–2015, a study was conducted by several hospitals to determine the safety of expressing colostrum prior to having a baby. The original study was for women with diabetes in pregnancy. It was called 'the DAME trial' and concluded that it was safe for women with diabetes in pregnancy, who were otherwise low risk, to express breast milk from 36 weeks, and that it caused no signs of harm to the mother or baby. It also concluded that babies were then more likely to only have breast milk while they were in hospital. Expressing colostrum is done by hand and not with a breast pump.

Check with your health care provider to see if there is anything in your medical history or any pregnancy related problems that would make expressing colostrum unsuitable for you.

Hand Expressing Technique

1. Gently massage the breasts prior to expressing.
2. Measure three fingers width up from the nipple base and place thumb here.
3. Place second and third fingers on the opposite side of the breast with the nipple lined up in the middle.
4. Press directly back into the breast with both fingers and thumb.
5. Now press finger and thumb together within the breast.
6. Roll (but not slide) the fingers forward within the breast towards the nipple.
7. The other hand holds the syringe or receptacle for the collection.

Refer to my website for a video of expressing milk by hand.

BREAST CHANGES
Through pregnancy, birth and beyond

Breasts are soft

Hormonal changes during pregnancy influence cells in the breast to make changes in preparation for milk production. After birth, when the placenta comes away, the hormones are no longer inhibiting breast milk production.

Small quantities of the first type of milk, called colostrum, is available at this time for your baby.

Breasts are firm and full

As you breastfeed with a comfortable attachment and you look and listen for the transfer of milk, your breasts respond by making milk to match your baby's appetite.

After birth, extra fluid within your body as well as the milk increasing in quantity (supply & demand) causes the breast to feel firm and full.

Breasts are alternating between firm and soft

As your body changes and your breasts become more efficient in producing milk, and with the changing needs of your baby, your breast will feel full prior to a feed and empty afterwards.

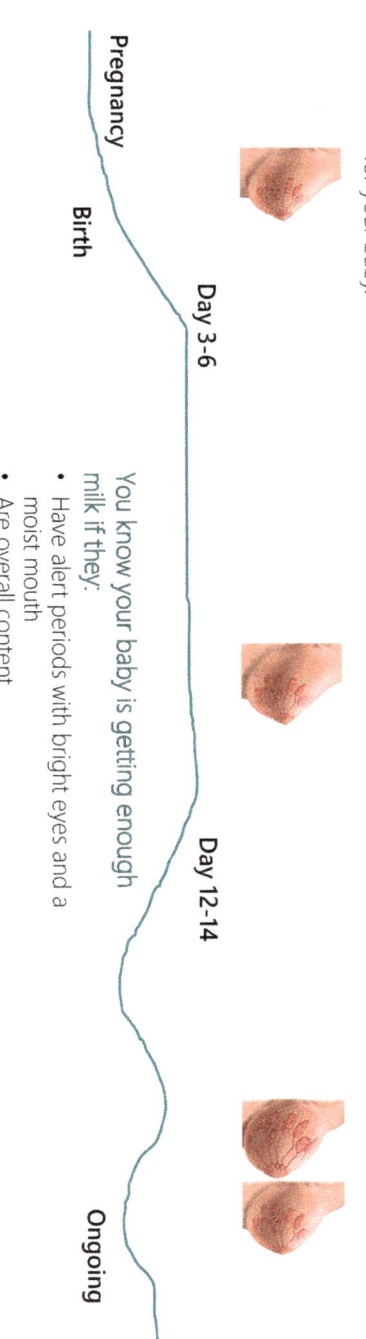

Pregnancy — Birth — Day 3-6 — Day 12-14 — Ongoing

You know your baby is getting enough milk if they:
- Have alert periods with bright eyes and a moist mouth
- Are overall content
- Have regular soaked nappies

www.motherandbaby-workinginharmony.com.au   Julie Jarrett RN, IBCLC, HPCE

When Your Baby is Born

Natural childbirth, wherever possible, is important for the benefit of both mother and child and enhances the breastfeeding experience. Educate yourself about natural childbirth and how best to achieve it. This may be through childbirth education classes, if you are having a hospital birth or accessing a childbirth practitioner privately who specialises in natural childbirth. See resource section for more information. Natural childbirth enables your hormonal system to work in a natural state, as nature intended.

Currently there is some fear around childbirth. This can result in a loss of confidence for the woman and her ability to birth well. Fear shuts down the body's natural ability to function efficiently when fight and flight hormones are released by the mother during labour. The uterus is not a priority during flight or fight, therefore there is a reduction in the amount of vital blood and oxygen received by the muscles of the uterus. Labour becomes longer, and the use of medical interventions is more likely.

There is a natural release of adrenalin in the final stages of birth, however, this is not caused by fight or flight instinct but is naturally present to assist the mother with the final efforts of birthing.

Immediately following birth, your baby lies directly upon your abdomen, her head near your heart.

The umbilical cord is still attached at this stage. It continues to pulsate, allowing the blood flow from the placenta to be received by your baby while your baby's lungs start to fill up with air. The vital oxygen continues to be received into your baby's system from the umbilical cord, as well as stem cells and other important nutrients such as iron.

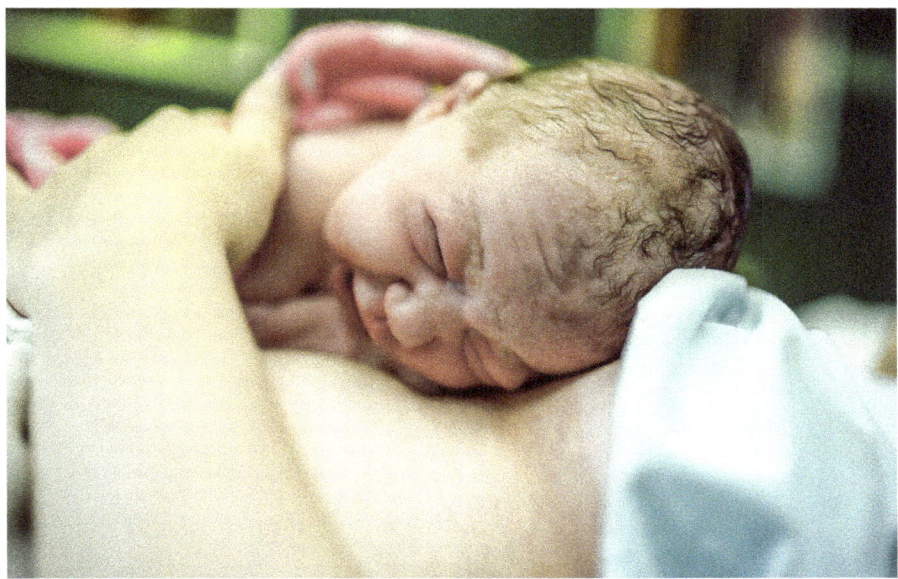

In the past, the baby's umbilical cord was clamped immediately following birth, however, scientific research now shows the benefits of delaying this process. When understanding this, you may wish to ensure that the carers in your birthing situation are aware of your wishes to delay cord clamping.

This is also an important time of quiet for the mother and her baby. If you think of yourself as the baby and you were coming into an environment of bright lights and noise, feeling cold and wet, it would not be very pleasant. Instead support her with your hands. Cover her in a warm blanket and quietly observe her.

At the beginning, her colour will go from a bluish tone to a beautiful pink colour as more oxygen enters her circulation. Her muscle tone will also increase.

In the first hour or so following birth, your baby is very alert, gazing around with eyes open. This is a time that mother and baby need quiet recovery time. Relaxed lighting and extra warmth for the mother will be beneficial. At the baby's own pace, she will start the journey to find the breast.

As the baby lies skin to skin, the mother will reach down to her newborn. The sharing of eye-to-eye contact and breathing in the smell of her baby, will release hormones such as oxytocin into her body. These hormones enhance the mother and baby's connection and assists the uterus to continue to contract, minimising blood loss.

As she lies on her mother's chest, she will at some point start to bob her head up and down, opening her mouth and moving her tongue forward. Her legs will push her up allowing her to navigate over to the area of the nipple and areola. She will use her hands to find her way as well.

The nipple area has little holes in it called follicles and they excrete an oil which smells similar to amniotic fluid. The baby will be attracted to the smell. This is such an important time, and the mother and baby should not feel like they are being rushed. Directly attaching to the breast can take over an hour to happen (the average time is 74 minutes). If the baby is able to find its way to the breast and attach successfully, it imprints into the baby's brain vital information, thus aiding her to attach well in follow up breastfeeds.

For some women, this process is made more difficult because of the way they are built. For example, women with large pendulous breasts or inverted nipples may require extra support and guidance.

At this point, it should also be noted that if a woman has received medication such as an epidural, pethidine or morphine during her labour, and especially if this has been given close to the birth, this may have an effect on her baby's ability to find and latch successfully onto the breast. It may just take a little more time for these babies.

Following the first breastfeed you may wish for your baby to be weighed. This needs to be done gently and quietly. Ensure some soft warm blankets made into a nest are placed on and weighed into the scales. If she is gently placed onto the scales this way, it should be a pleasant experience.

When you are getting up for a shower, your partner may like to take the baby onto their chest, skin to skin. Your baby is continuing to be reassured that they are safe and cared for. When a baby is unsupported and lying on their back, they have a startle reflex, called a Moro reflex, which can be disturbing to them. A supported position or skin to skin contact helps prevent this.

When you are bathing yourself after the birth, be conscious of what products (if any) you use. Soaps, deodorants, and shampoos can wash off the scent of the amniotic fluid. The fluid scent on your chest enables your baby to find her way back to the breast for feeding. Also, your baby's sense of smell will be sensitive to strong, artificial odours.

Ongoing Breastfeeding

Understanding the size of a baby's stomach will give you the confidence to know that in the early days of your baby's life, only small quantities of colostrum are needed.

Colostrum is a thick fluid that ranges from clear to yellow/orange in colour. It supplies your baby with nutrition and

How big is your baby's stomach

1 MONTH

Size of an egg

80-150ml
2.5-5oz

1 WEEK

Size of an apricot

45-60ml
1.5-2oz

DAY 2

Size of a walnut

22-27ml
.75-1oz

DAY 1

Size of a Cherry

5-7ml
1-1.4 teaspoons

www.motherandbaby-workinginharmony.com.au

immune factors. These immune qualities of colostrum are especially important as your baby has a greater need for immune protection in the early days of their life.

When the quantity of milk increases it is yellow in colour until it becomes mature milk. Mature milk ranges from a bluish shade to white.

TIPS

 Continuing milk production is determined by the removal of milk from your breast based on your baby's appetite and each breast has a different experience of milk production.

 There is a protein in breast milk called F.I.L. (Feedback Inhibitor of Lactation). When a breast is full with lots of this protein present, the breast milk production is slow. If the breast is emptied, production of milk becomes more rapid.

Larger capacity breast = emptied less frequently = slower milk production

Smaller capacity breasts = emptied more frequently = more rapid production

If you ever believe that your supply of breast milk is low:
- ∞ Make sure your attachment is deep.
- ∞ Feed your baby from both breasts, draining them well.
- ∞ If you decide to use a pump to increase the supply, if possible, wait an hour after the breast feed before pumping rather than straight away. This allows the breast to begin to refill.

Further Information for Breastfeeding

I have worked with many women over the years helping them with their breastfeeding experiences. I have developed some easy-to-follow ways of teaching women breastfeeding skills that I wish to share with you. For babies, breastfeeding is instinctive. For women, it is a learned skill. In our modern world we have limited opportunities to observe other women breastfeeding.

If you are experiencing difficulties, always go back to the skin-to-skin position with your baby placed on your chest, lying between your breasts. While you are gaining confidence, create a private warm area where you won't be disturbed. A bare chest is better for when you are learning, as clothing tends to get in the way and can be distracting.

Sit in a supportive chair. If the back of the chair is very upright, place a pillow behind your back so that you can achieve a supportive angle with your body when you lean back. A footstool is also helpful to keep your lap supported so that your thighs are parallel to the ground.

Baby Language and Feeding Cues

Before you start breastfeeding your baby, it is important to understand their language and cues for feeding.

Easy Ways to Understand Breastfeeding Techniques

Skin to Skin Down to Cradle Position

As your baby starts to wake, she will show the signs of hunger. Bring her to your chest, skin to skin, and when she is ready, she will start to slowly move down towards the breast.

BABY LANGUAGE

At first, you may not understand your little one's language and cues, but as you get to know your baby in the days and weeks after they are born, you will begin to recognise the signs that will tell you when they are hungry, ready for a feed or happy to engage.

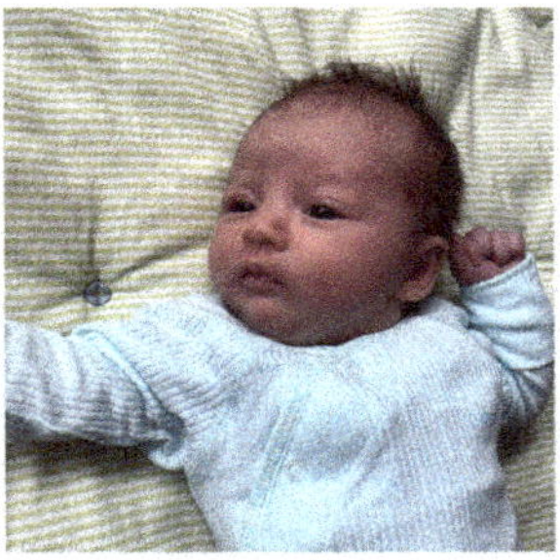

HAPPY BABY	WANTING TO ENGAGE	STIRRING/STRETCHING
TURNING	MOUTH OPEN	HAND TO MOUTH
LATE FEEDING SIGN	WINDY	READY FOR SLEEP

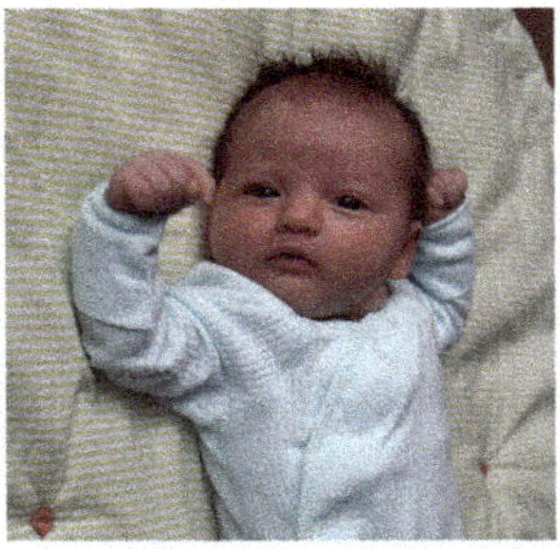

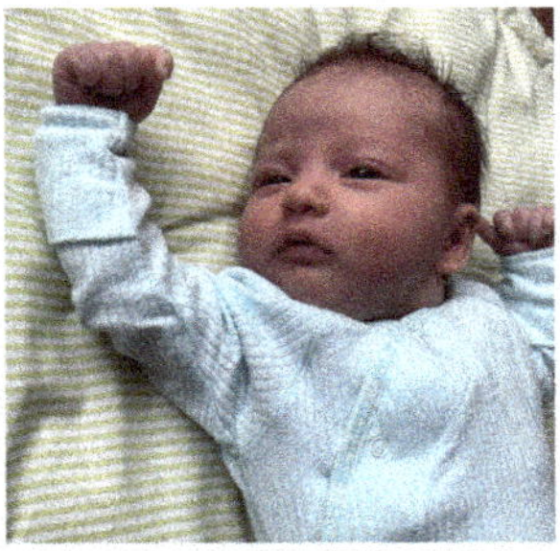

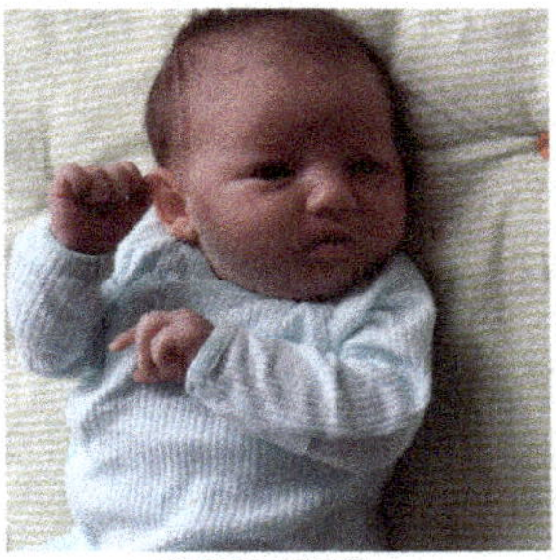

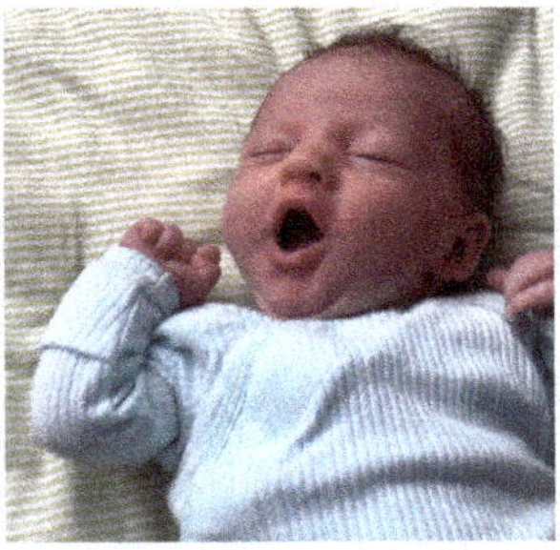

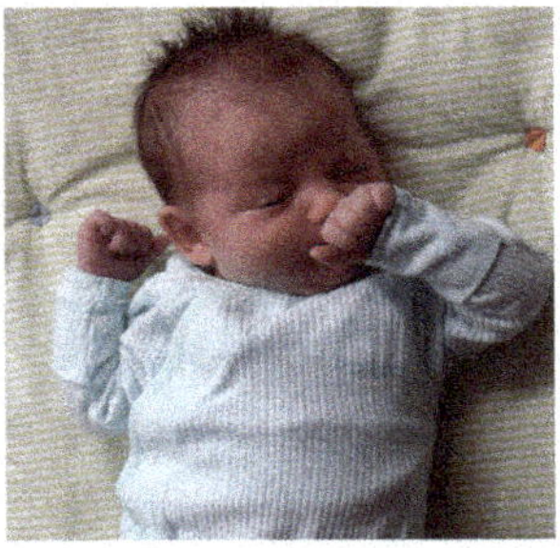

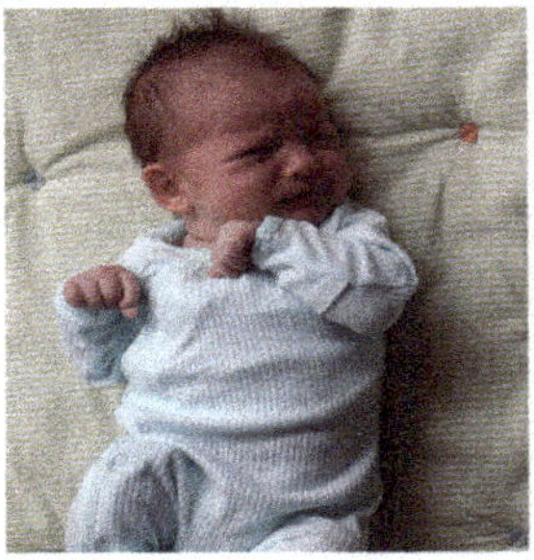

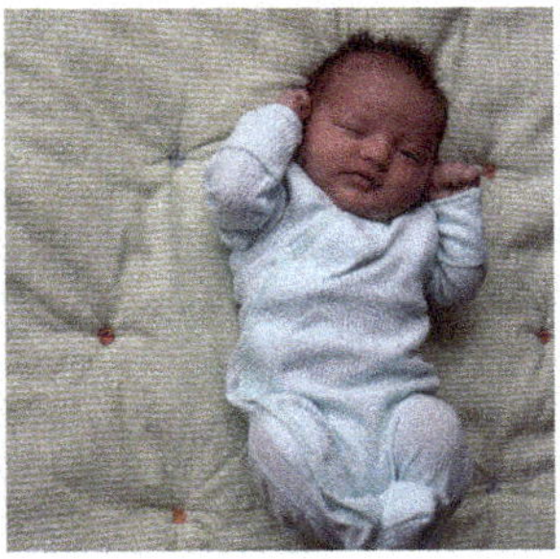

If your baby has become stressed or reached the stage of showing the late feeding sign, it will be beneficial to comfort and relax them first before feeding. This will be a much more pleasant experience for you and your baby.

www.motherandbaby-workinginharmony.com.au   Julie Jarrett RM, IBCLC

This method of attaching your baby to the breast will be easiest when you are sitting down in a comfortable chair with your body angled backwards to support your baby. Place a pillow in the small of your back to achieve this. This example is for the baby going to the right breast.

1. Support her back and neck area with your left hand.
2. Use your right hand to gently nudge her hips across under your left breast.
3. As her body becomes more parallel to the ground, gather her body with your left arm.
4. Slide your right hand to your right breast and support your breast, in the shape of a "C" with the thumb landing **opposite** where your baby's nose is.

5. Her head and shoulders need to slope back so that the chin is the first part of her face to touch the breast. Holding your baby comfortably behind the neck, shoulders, and back, and not behind the head ensures the chin touches the breast first.

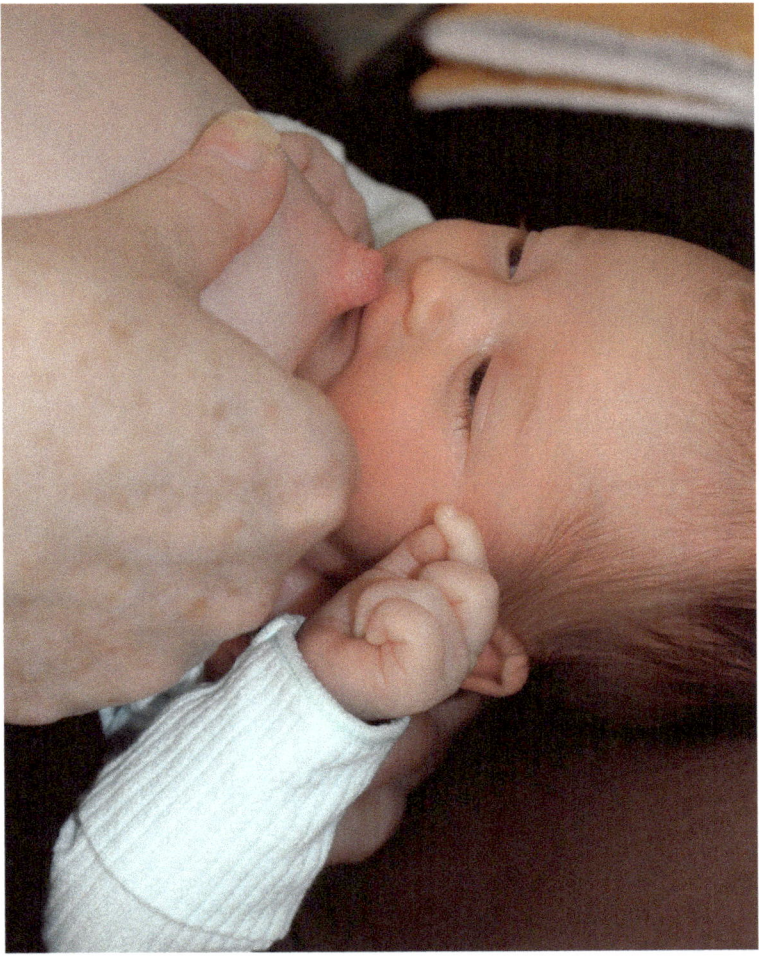

6. Whilst her mouth is still closed, the nipple will be pointed up towards her nose, just **above** the top lip.

7. When her mouth opens wide, nudge her directly forward into your chest through her shoulders and back (not the head).

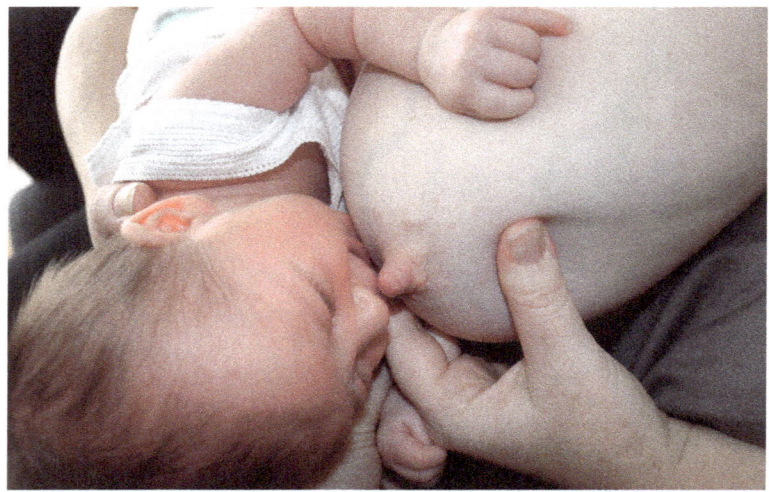

8. At the **exact** moment you nudge her forward through the shoulders and back, press your thumb into the breast tissue. This allows the nipple to be taken deeply into the baby's mouth.

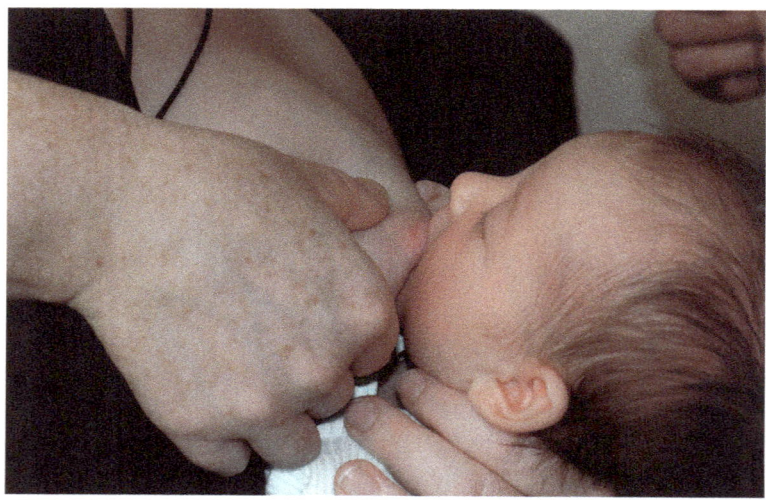

9. Hold this position until your baby has established a good feeding rhythm.

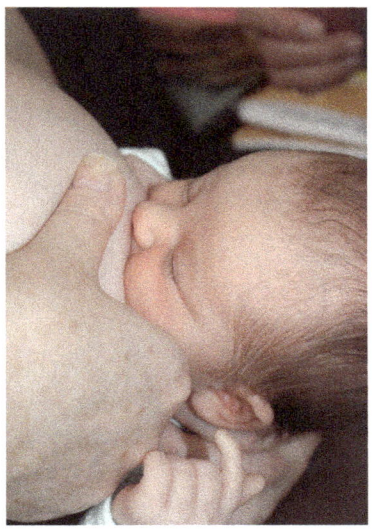

10. While watching your baby and breast, slowly lower your right hand down until you no longer feel any weight of your breast in this hand.

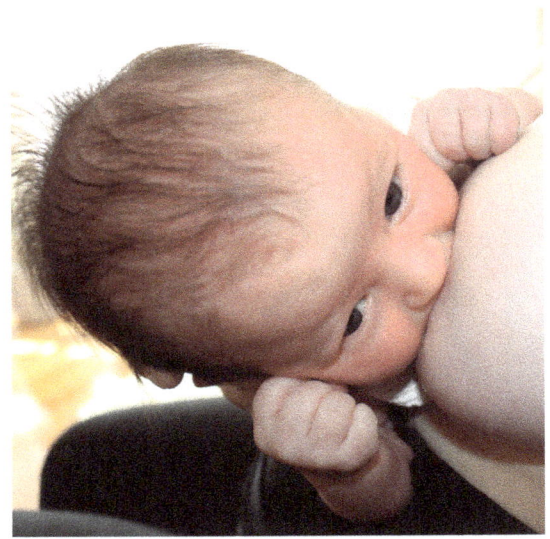

11. Now bring your right hand around to cradle the baby. When you get more confident, you will be able to move your left hand out, which will now be free for you to access food and drink if required.

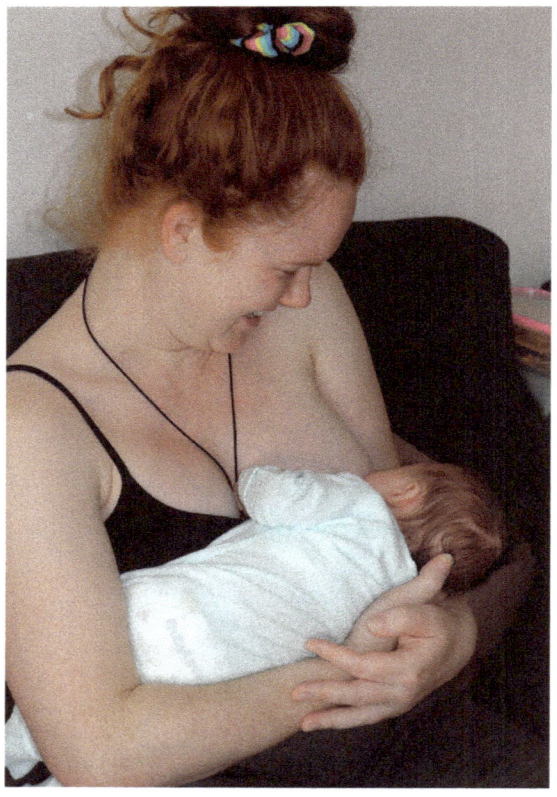

The importance of the chin touching the breast is that babies have built in reflexes in this area that encourages their mouth to open widely.

Without the chin touching, a baby gets confused and will swing their head side to side, searching.

Breastfeeding Attachment

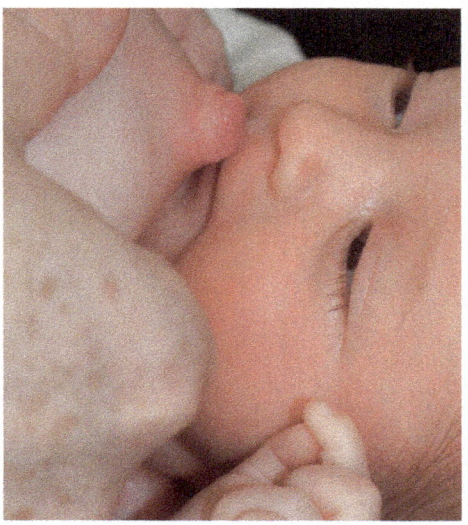

Whilst her mouth is still closed, the nipple will be pointed up towards her nose, just above the top lip.

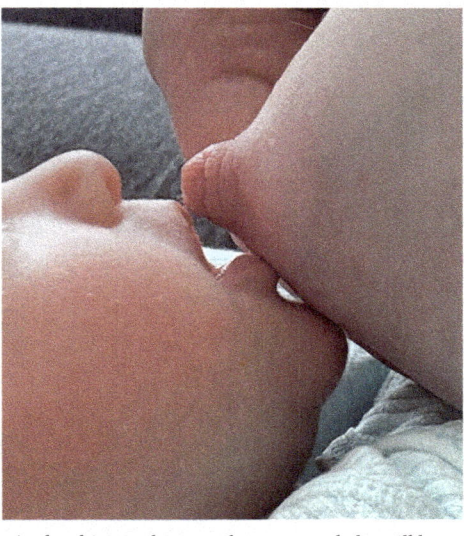

As the chin touches your breast, your baby will be prompted to open her mouth

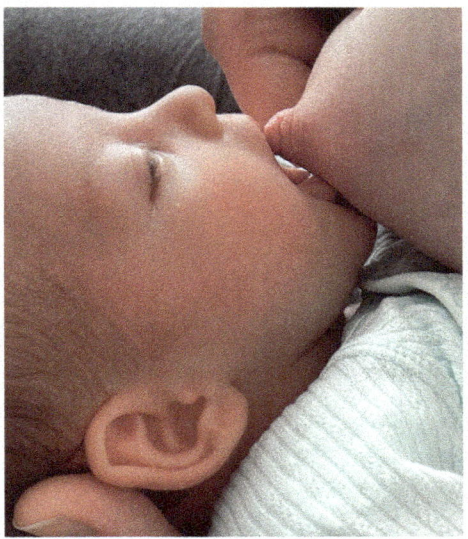

When her mouth opens wide, nudge her directly forward into your breast, through her shoulders and back (not the head).

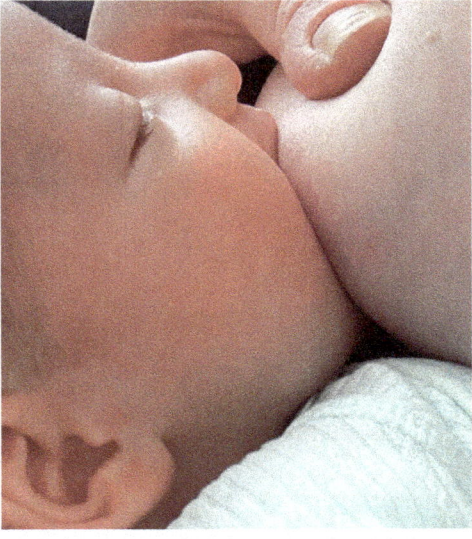

At the exact moment you nudge her forward, press your thumb into the breast tissue. This allows the nipple to be taken deeply into the baby's mouth.

Remember once your baby is comfortably attached and feeding, reposition your arms to cradle your baby.

www.motherandbaby-workinginharmony.com.au   Julie Jarrett RM, IBCLC

Shallow, painful latch

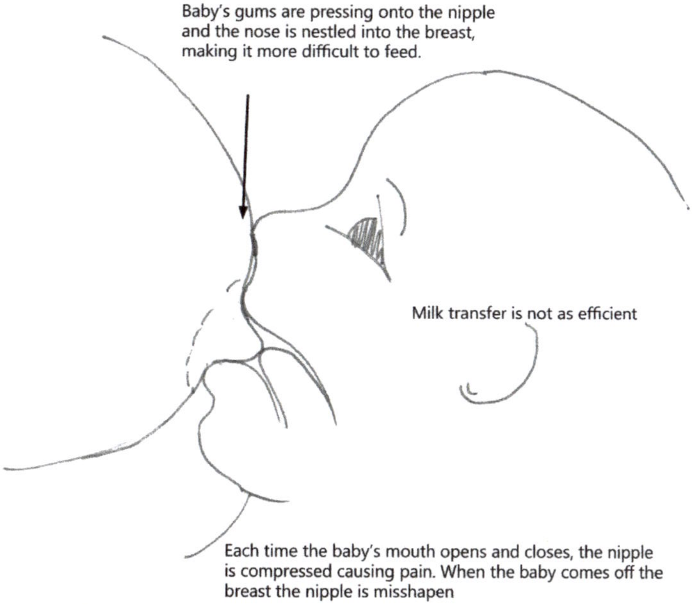

Baby's gums are pressing onto the nipple and the nose is nestled into the breast, making it more difficult to feed.

Milk transfer is not as efficient

Each time the baby's mouth opens and closes, the nipple is compressed causing pain. When the baby comes off the breast the nipple is misshapen

Deep comfortable latch

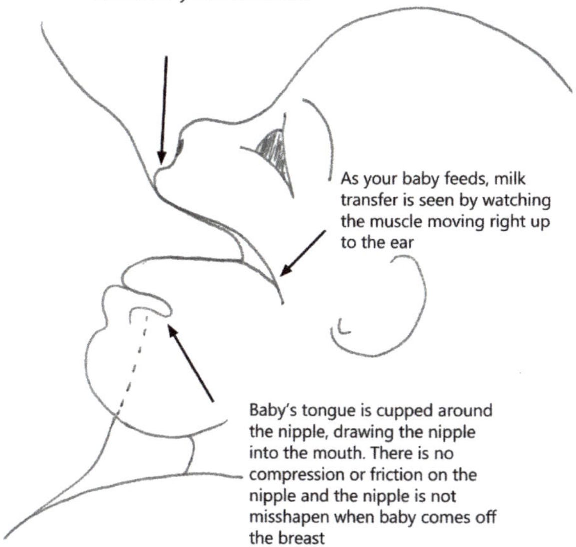

Baby's gums nestled around the areola and the nose is away from the breast

As your baby feeds, milk transfer is seen by watching the muscle moving right up to the ear

Baby's tongue is cupped around the nipple, drawing the nipple into the mouth. There is no compression or friction on the nipple and the nipple is not misshapen when baby comes off the breast

www.motherandbaby-workinginharmony.com.au

If attachment is good and deep it will feel comfortable and pain free. If you are working on the technique above and you have some existing nipple damage, you may feel uncomfortable in the beginning, however, this sensation will quickly settle down as the feed progresses and the attachment is correct.

If there is a continuing pinching sensation, place your finger gently into the side of her mouth to release some air. Take your baby off the breast and start again. You will know that you have achieved good attachment on the breast when:

1. The attachment is pain free.
2. The nipple shape after your baby has finished feeding will be round and normal (not misshapen).
3. You see your baby feeding with deep rhythmic sucks followed by pauses. You will see this through the action in her jaw, and you may hear the swallowing.

Other Positions

Underarm Position

This position works well for women with larger, more pendulous breasts.

The steps are exactly the same as the cradle position, however, the baby is now lying under your breast while being wrapped around your waist. Keep your arm straight and your baby supported. Then, slide your baby back under the breast, so that your baby is looking up at your breast.

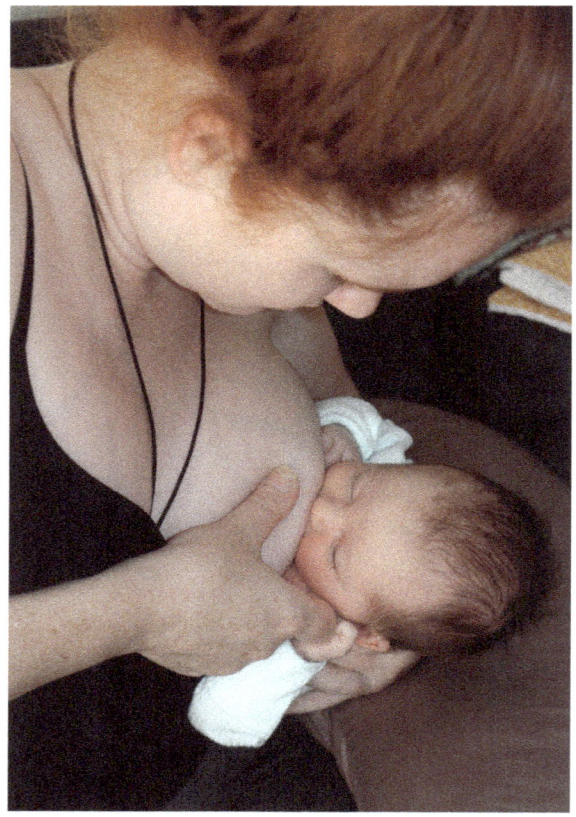

Remove your right hand once feeding is established, otherwise pressure on the breast from the thumb can block milk ducts.

Side Lying Position

This position will be good for women who find sitting down uncomfortable after birth, or need a position in which to relax in.

In this position you will be lying down on your side with your body bent forward in the middle.

Make sure the baby is looking up toward the breast and nipple, not into the breast. The setup will be the same as the cradle position from step 6–9.

More Helpful Information for Breastfeeding

When your milk starts to come into the breast in increasing quantities, usually around the third or fourth day following birth, it is a good idea to start to fully empty the first breast you start feeding on, before going to the other breast. The reason behind this is that the breast milk increases in its fat content as the breast empties, and you don't want your baby to miss out on the important nutritional properties of these fats. It also gives your breast the message of how much it needs to fill up for following feeds (supply and demand).

It may look something like this: your baby is starting to stir with the mouth moving and the fist going up to the mouth.

You scoop her up and guide her onto the first side (breast A). She attaches well, and you observe milk transfer.

She drifts into a sleepy state at some time during the feed, and she either let's go of the breast or you observe her sucking quietly with non-milk transfer and you guide her off. You bring her up gently into a vertical supported position to allow her wind to escape. Changing her nappy now will start to wake her up again, which will give her the opportunity to be placed back onto the same side (breast A) to fully drain this breast.

Once breast A feels drained, if your baby is looking for more, transfer her to the other breast (side B), until she is completely relaxed and content.

For the next feed reverse this i.e., start the feed on side B.

Milk transfer is when milk is coming from your breast into your baby's mouth and is swallowed. You will be able to see this happening by looking at the muscle that goes from the corner of the mouth to the ear. The whole muscle will be moving in a rhythmic way.

Non milk transfer is when a baby is suckling on the breast with a gentler motion. You will see the mouth and the area near the mouth moving but not the whole muscle to the ear. Very little, if any, swallowing will be heard.

TIP

For ease of working out which side to start the feed on, place a hair tie around your wrist. This will indicate which side you would start the feed on. When you change your baby's nappy, change the hair tie to the other wrist.

Change the Baby, Change the Hair Tie

The next feed will come along, and you will know easily which is the correct breast to start on. This is a handy tip especially in the middle of the night.

If you are forgetting to change the hair tie, place a 'sticky note' on the baby's change mat so that each time you or your partner changes your baby's nappy, you are reminded to change the hair tie onto the other wrist.

Burping Your Baby

Your baby has many changes occurring in their gut prior to and after they are born. This includes swallowing the amniotic fluid, ingesting colostrum, and coming in contact with new bacteria in their environment. While a mother and baby are learning to feed, excessive air is often introduced into the baby's stomach if the attachment or seal around the baby's mouth is incomplete.

A combination of factors helps create a buildup of air. A baby will indicate when they have been unable to release this excessive air by looking uncomfortable in their body, drawing their legs up towards the chest, or behaving in a restless manner.

A newborn baby relies on us to assist them to release this air. Often all that is required is a change of position, such as bringing them up into a supported position onto your shoulder. Just like a bottle of soda water that is lying on its side, picking up the bottle makes all the bubbles head up to the top.

A cycle of your baby crying and in pain may cause you to put your baby back onto the breast. Babies who are in pain can look hungry, as they use their fists to suck on, to comfort themselves. The difference between hunger and pain is that when they are in pain the rest of their body will look uncomfortable as well. If the previous feed is still undigested, this can create more discomfort for the baby.

Another method to help release the buildup of wind is to sit your baby up onto your lap, well supported between your two hands. To do this keep the trunk of their body straight and then slightly lean them forward onto one hand, with the other hand on their back. Keep them close to you so that they can see you and feel secure. Add gentle rhythmic taps over their back with part of your tapping hand remaining in contact with them. Babies love you moving while you hold them so adding slow rhythmic movements can be very calming. You will find the right movements of your body; it will come naturally after a little while.

 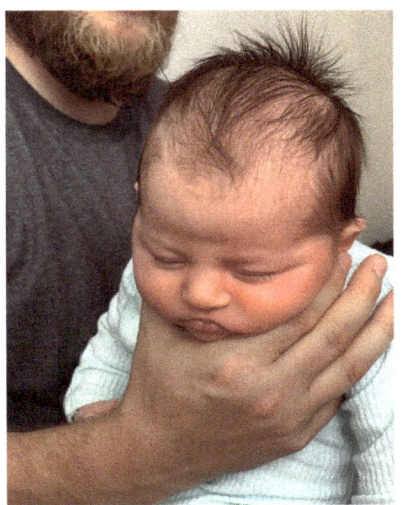

Other things that may help are a warm relaxing bath, a gentle tummy rub, or carefully moving their legs up and down while they are lying on your lap or on a change mat.

Many babies bring up milk after a feed. Generally, this is not a concern. It can be caused by you having an abundant milk supply and a rapid release of the milk at the beginning of the feed your baby can't keep up with. For some babies, the area at the top of their stomach needs more time to mature to keep the milk in place.

Overall, it might just be a laundry problem, i.e., lots of clothes to wash.

If you are unsure, or have any concerns, then seek out your trusted healthcare worker.

TIP

 When you experience seeing a baby bring up milk during or after a feed, it can look like they have brought up all their feed, when in fact, it may only be a small amount. A good exercise to do is to measure 5–10mls of milk and spread it over a surface. This will give you an idea of how a small amount can seem like a lot.

How Much Milk?

I often get asked the question, "how do I know if my baby is getting enough milk?" There are a few easy ways to tell:

1. First off, check the amount of urine that is in your baby's nappy. I would expect for a one-week-old baby, five or so wet nappies in 24 hours. The nappies would feel heavy when you hold them in your hand. The urine would be clear in colour, not concentrated.
2. Then the bowel actions. A one-week-old baby will have a yellow mustard coloured bowel action, producing one or more within 24 hours. Generally, as a baby gets a lot older, they will have days (or longer) between having bowel movements. All babies differ with what is normal for them.
3. Observe your baby on the breast. In the first few days of life the sucking will be in an irregular type of pattern. Around the third and fourth day you should be able to see a different pattern of sucking occurring as more milk is coming into the breast. You should be able to hear your baby swallowing the milk as well. Your baby's stomach size is increasing, and their gut is becoming relaxed and moving more.
4. During your baby's wakeful moments, they will look bright and alert with good muscle tone.

5. When your baby is weighed on the third day of life, they will generally have lost between 5%–8% of their birth weight. After that time, they will start gaining weight at approximately 20–30 grams per day, reaching back to their birth weight at around two weeks of age. By three months of age, the weight gain may start to slow down as those first months of life is a period of rapid growth and development. This is a general guide only as babies are all different. If you have any concerns regarding your baby's health, visit your trusted healthcare provider.

TIPS

 A healthcare provider is someone that you can develop confidence and trust in. You should feel as though they have time for you, and you don't feel rushed through the appointment. You should feel confident to ask them any question that is of concern to you. They will be someone who is willing to answer your questions with good quality information behind their answers. If you are unable to develop that sort of relationship with your healthcare provider, then it is your choice to find somebody else who you can develop that trusted relationship with. You and your baby deserve this.

Write down any questions before you go to your appointment.

How Long to Breast Feed For?

Ideally a baby is breast fed exclusively for six-months, with continued breastfeeding once solid foods are introduced. Continuing breastfeeding for up to two years or longer is ideal. This will be determined by the mother and baby's needs.

Around **six months** of age, physical changes allow a baby to sit up with less support and with increased head control present. The mouth size increases structurally and the fat pads inside the mouth reabsorb. Muscular development occurs around the tongue and lips. The coordination of muscles allow food to move in and around the mouth, directing the food to the back part of the tongue in preparation to swallow. If they receive food too early, these changes may not be sufficiently present. Please remember that every baby is different and will start solid foods at different stages.

When they are ready to start eating foods of appropriate consistency for the age and development of the baby, breast feed first before the food.

Should my Baby be Fed on a Schedule or Demand Fed?

Babies have built-in (instinctive) appetite indicators so they will know when they are hungry and when they are satisfied.

Just like us adults, if we eat when we are not overly hungry, we find that our food does not digest well. When our stomach is empty, we experience the feeling of hunger and eat food that digests well.

On page 140, I tell the story of a woman who was waking up her two and half month old baby during the day wanting her to feed more often with the aim of having her sleep longer at night. This created digestive upsets in her baby. Babies do not know what a clock is, so it is irrelevant to them what time it is.

There are times in the early days of life when it is appropriate to wake your baby for a feed. For example, if they are born premature, or if they are extra sleepy from the medications received at the birth. Babies who become increasingly jaundiced (yellow colour of the skin), or who have insufficient weight gains may need scheduled feeds, however, when these problems resolve, feeding on demand would be appropriate.

Babies have small stomachs and do require frequent feeds when they are very young. As they get older, the stomach size increases therefore the time gaps between feeds become longer. Also, they are more efficient with their feeding as they get older and stronger, and the actual time spent feeding at the breast is a lot less.

When Breastmilk is Unable to Meet the Needs of Your Baby

In the early days and weeks, if there is insufficient milk to supply the needs of your baby, your baby will have lower than expected urine or bowel output, will look hungry, and will be unsatisfied after feeds. They will also have low weight gain or weight losses. It is important to give your baby extra milk to help them gain more energy so that they are able to feed more efficiently and for longer periods of time. Seeking help from a professional health care provider who specialises in baby care is important to assist you in finding solutions.

As a Lactation Consultant, many mothers come to me in this situation, often feeling disappointed, frustrated, and needing lots of support. Together we look at all aspects of their breastfeeding, up until the present time. A baby check will pick up any structural concerns, such as tongue ties, that may be contributing to the situation. Often, when watching a feed, the answers will become clear. It may be that your baby may not be attached to the breast deeply enough. When the attachment is more superficial, the baby can get breast milk, however, they will be working harder to get sufficient milk for their needs, thus tiring more easily.

After some teaching and guidance, when the baby attaches deeper onto the breast, the mother can see and feel the difference. The baby will not be coming on and off the breast and will show a different sucking and swallowing pattern. After the feed, the baby will look satisfied and be in a deep relaxed state. There will be no pain in the nipples or breast, and the nipple will not be misshapen straight after the feed. The breast will feel drained in a different way than before, and any areas that the mother feels in her breast that have felt thickened or lumpy, will start to soften. This will also increase the supply of breast milk.

Until your supply increases, if your baby requires extra milk, express breastmilk by hand or use a quality breast pump. Allow about an hour after a breastfeed to express, as this gives the breast the opportunity to start filling up again.

TIPS

 Having the expressed milk available ahead of a feed will take the stress out of having a hungry baby who is restless or is starting to get fussy about going onto the breast. Having some available expressed milk to give before the attachment will allow a more relaxed effort onto the breast.

Smaller quantities of milk can be given via a cup or spoon, encouraging the continued confidence of the baby's ability to attach to the breast. Larger quantities of milk may need to be given via a bottle. Some babies will manage well with both a bottle and a breastfeed, however, some babies may become confused between the two.

Women who are experiencing ongoing insufficient breastmilk, may benefit from using a supply line. A bottle that contains expressed breast milk, or a breast milk substitute, is suspended around the mother's neck. As the baby starts to successfully attach onto the breast, the mother slides the tubing into the side of the baby's mouth. The baby will potentially stay on the breast for longer periods of time, gaining confidence in breastfeeding and stimulating the mother's supply as well.

A woman who finds herself with insufficient breast milk for her baby, can find this to be an emotionally difficult time, and will require support from family, friends, and health carers. She may require some medical investigations, for example to check for hormonal imbalances, or some sessions with a breastfeeding specialist who is known as a Lactation Consultant. Whatever is required must be done to give the mother the answers she needs, and hopefully, effective solutions.

Other contributors to a reduced or absent breastmilk supply can be hormonal imbalances, anatomy challenges such as inverted nipples, some types of breast surgeries, or ongoing stress factors. Seek medical assistance if this condition continues.

Some Considerations of Vitamins and Minerals for Mother and Baby Health

Wherever possible our vitamins and minerals need to be derived from a well-balanced variety of foods that come from soils which are healthy, alive in microorganisms, and rich in mineral components.

Some vitamins in breastmilk, such as vitamin A, B12, C, D, and K, are influenced by the mother's intake.

VITAMIN A

Vitamin A is a fat-soluble vitamin, and it is necessary for vision and to support the immune system.

Mother: Good food sources are from fruits (dried and fresh), vegetables (yellow and green) and animal sources such as eggs.

Baby: Breast milk is an excellent source of vitamin A, especially in early lactation if the mother's intake is adequate.

VITAMIN B'S (eight different water-soluble B vitamins)

The B vitamins play a role in cell metabolism (changing food to energy), maintenance of the central nervous system, supporting the immune system and the making of red blood cells.

Mother: The vitamin B's are available in a wide range of foods such as bananas, avocados and other fruits, green vegetables, sweet potatoes and other vegetables, lentils and animal sources such as tuna and eggs.

B12 (Cobalamin) may be deficient in women who have a vegan (non-animal product) eating plan or a restricted vegetarian plan. These mothers will need to include foods that are fortified with vitamin B12 e.g., fortified almond milk or by taking a vitamin B12 supplement.

Baby: Breastmilk is influenced by a mother's uptake of this vitamin. If breastmilk is deficient in B12, the baby can show signs such as weakness, low muscle tone, delay in development, fatigue, and failure to thrive.

VITAMIN C

Our bodies are dependent upon external sources of vitamin C, as we cannot make our own.

Mother: Vitamin C is found in fruits and vegetables and is higher when these foods are in their raw form.

Baby: Intake for the baby is dependent upon the content in the breast milk which will be adequate if the mother has a sufficient intake of fresh fruits and vegetables.

VITAMIN D

Vitamin D is essential for bone growth and supports our physical and mental well-being. It also supports our immune system.

Mother: Sunlight reacting on the skin is the major natural source of vitamin D. Only a few foods have vitamin D in them, foods such as fatty fish, eggs and some varieties of mushrooms.

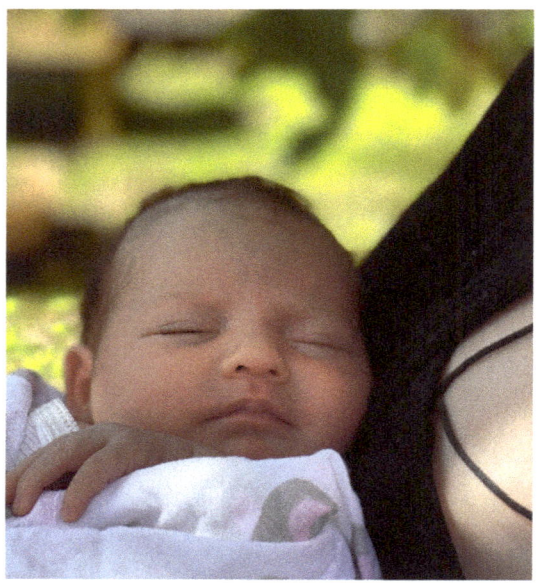

A mother will be at risk of low vitamin D levels from some of the following lifestyle factors: having limited sensible exposure to sunlight due to working and living indoors, wearing clothing that excludes sunlight, constant use of sunscreen (consider sensible sunning instead), having limited exposure to sunlight due to seasonal changes or living in polluted cities.

A blood test can check your vitamin D levels and if you are unable to increase your exposure to sunlight, supplementation may be required.

Baby: If a baby has normal vitamin D stores these may become depleted by two-months of age in the absence of any sensible exposure to sunlight.

VITAMIN E (fat soluble vitamin)

Vitamin E, as an antioxidant, protects the cell membrane (outermost covering of a cell) from damage.

Mother: Vitamin E is found in foods such as green leafy vegetables (spinach, broccoli), seeds (sunflower), nuts (almonds) and oils (olive oil).

Baby: Colostrum and mature breast milk are high in vitamin E. Premature and growth restricted babies have low levels of vitamin E at birth.

VITAMIN K

Vitamin K is important for its blood clotting factors.

Mother: Vitamin K is derived from plant sources such as leafy green vegetables, avocados, and kiwi fruit.

Baby: Concentration in breast milk varies and is dependent on the mother's intake.

Some babies are prone to a deficiency in vitamin K in the early days and weeks of their life. Low levels can cause a bleeding disorder known as vitamin K deficiency bleeding. Ensure your baby receives early feedings of colostrum, you are consuming foods that are high in this vitamin, and educate yourself on early supplementation of vitamin K for babies.

In the reference section of this book, there is a book by Dr Sarah Wickham, giving the reader information about vitamin K and your newborn.

MINERALS

Breast milk has the necessary amounts of minerals to keep all your baby's body systems functioning normally. Generally, the concentration of minerals in breastmilk is largely unaffected by dietary intake.

CALCIUM

Mother: A lactating woman who is eating well will have sufficient calcium available in her breastmilk. Calcium levels in a mother's bones (bone mineral density) reduces during breastfeeding, however these levels recover once her baby weans off the breast. Some examples of plant foods which are rich in calcium are leafy green vegetables such as spinach, kale, watercress, and Chinese cabbage. Fruits such as oranges and dried figs are also a good source, as well as nuts such as almonds.

Baby: Calcium for the baby is required for bone growth and regulating the heart and muscle function. Breast milk calcium levels are not changed if a mother is given calcium supplements while lactating, however, if a woman is low on calcium during pregnancy and takes extra calcium, then this may have an influence on the levels in the breast milk.

IRON

Mother: A deficiency can occur if a woman's intake is too low to replace the amount of iron lost from the body every day. A deficiency in iron can lead to symptoms such as fatigue. Foods that are rich in iron may include vegetables such as spinach and broccoli, red meat, pumpkin seeds, quinoa and legumes such as chickpeas, peas and beans. If a mother is deficient in iron, generally her breastmilk will have sufficient iron for her baby's needs.

Baby: The presence of high lactose and vitamin C in breastmilk helps with the absorption of the iron.

When a baby has grown sufficiently and is ready to commence the addition of foods alongside breastfeeding (generally from six months of age and beyond), the foods they receive will need to include foods that are rich in iron.

ZINC

Mother: Sufficient zinc is required for enzyme activity, wound healing, protein and DNA synthesis, cell division and immune function. Daily consumption of foods that contain zinc is important as zinc is not stored in the body. Some foods that are rich in zinc are seafood, lentils, nuts, seeds (consider sprouting them to increase their bioavailability) and meat. Fruit and vegetables contain some zinc but not at high levels.

Baby: Reduced growth, and poor functioning of the immune system and loss of appetite, can occur if there is insufficient zinc available for a baby.

IODINE

Mother: The foods richest in iodine come from the ocean (fish and seaweed). Some brands of salt contain some iodine. Iodine is required for making thyroid hormones.

Baby: A deficiency of iodine can impact on a baby's brain development. Iodine levels in breastmilk can vary widely, depending on a mother's dietary intake, and the level of iodine in the soil that food is grown in. The levels in the soil can vary significantly with different geographical areas.

MAGNESIUM

Mother: Magnesium is a mineral that is essential for many of the chemical reactions that constantly take place in our bodies.

It is found in the bones, muscles, soft tissues and body fluids. Insufficient magnesium can have many health implications ranging from muscle cramps, irregular heartbeat and poor bone health.

Foods such as fruits, nuts, vegetables and wholegrains should provide sufficient levels, however, factors such as chemical farming methods, food processing, dieting, and stress can have an effect on the amount of magnesium available.

Baby: Healthy eating by the mother to include foods rich in magnesium will ensure an adequate intake in the breastmilk for the baby.

Your Baby's Healthy Immune System

WE ARE EXPOSED to trillions of microbes (a microscopic organism too small for the naked eye to see) every day. The human body has an immune system which performs many processes, checks and balances so that we function normally, with health and vitality. The immune system is not in one area of the body but throughout it. The complex immune system is made up of specialised cells, tissues, organs, and proteins (white blood cells, bone marrow, lymph nodes, tonsils, thymus, spleen).

Supporting our overall health is important for an optimal functioning immune system:

∞ Avoiding excessive stress.
∞ Making good healthy food choices.
∞ Avoiding harmful chemicals in your daily life (cleaning products, personal care products, food additives).
∞ Obtaining food that comes from soils that are rich, pesticide free, and alive in microorganisms.

- Staying well hydrated by drinking water uncontaminated by chemicals and pollutants.
- Allowing yourself plenty of time to enjoy the benefits of being out in nature, with fresh air, sunshine, and exercise.

Our bodies are amazing in how well they can repair themselves when given the opportunity, even if they have suffered a lot of neglect. It is a joy to get up in the morning and move with energy and freedom. You deserve to feel great and if you do not, start by making changes right now. Being healthy, by supporting a strong immune system before you are pregnant, when pregnant, and as a new mother, has amazing benefits for you and your baby.

Understanding Your Baby's Immune System

Your baby's immune system will have developed during the pregnancy. Once she is born, this immature but complete system continues to develop rapidly through an ongoing process. The initial response comes mainly from the gut flora of the mother. As a baby is being born vaginally, she will pick up bacteria and other microorganisms that has come from her mother's gut. As she is placed onto the mother's chest, skin to skin, she contacts her mother's skin flora as well.

At birth, the baby's gut is relatively sterile and the exposure to the mother's intestinal and skin bacteria sets up and establishes (colonises) a healthy gut flora. With the aid of breastmilk, beneficial bacteria such as bifidobacterial and lactobacilli are established in the baby's gut. Bacteria such as these have a symbiotic (mutually beneficial) relationship to humans, promoting good digestion, boosting the immune system, regulating a healthy gut pH, and inhibiting non-beneficial, harmful bacteria or fungal overgrowth.

Previous maternity practices of enemas, cleansing the perineum (the area between the vagina and the anus), and draping the area with sterile drapes prior to birth are generally no longer practiced.

Understanding the importance of how the newborn develops its immune system allows us to enhance and protect this process around birth. Supporting a vaginal birth, whenever possible, and being comfortable that contact with the bacteria from the mother's perineum and skin is actually beneficial. The need to support birthing environments that are peaceful, calm, dimly lit, and with women educated, empowered, and encouraged to birth in upright positions (whenever possible) will enhance the process. Delaying the cutting of the cord following birth allows an abundance of stem cells to be available for the baby. Extensive skin to skin time without unnecessary interruptions is also important.

Initially, handling a baby by anyone else but the mother and the father followed then by close family members, is best for the baby in the early days following birth. If anyone other than the parents need to handle the newborn, they need to use strict hygiene so that no one else's skin flora is establishing in the baby's gut. The mother's breastmilk will give protection from micro-organisms common to her skin and intestines, but not to others that she is not colonised with. This information is for the early stage of your baby's life. As your baby's immune system matures, human interactions with other family members and friends close to the parents is appropriate.

The rich protective factors of breastmilk come in the form of specific proteins, carbohydrates, fats and other cellular components.

One example is a protein called secretory immunoglobulin (SIgA). This protein is particularly high in colostrum, providing your baby with immediate protection from microbes following birth. It also provides targeted protection, which means that if a mother comes into contact with a particular harmful bacterium via her lungs (breathing it in), or gut (digesting it in), then her system immediately responds. The harmful bacterium hits specific tissue areas in her lungs or gut, creating sensitised cells that then travel via her lymph and blood systems to various areas in her body, including the breasts. Anti-bodies are created and ingested by the baby via the breast milk. This process gives the baby rapid and specific protection from a harmful bacterium that the mother and baby came in contact with. How amazing!

Another protein is called lactoferrin. It has many functions, including being a bactericide (kills bacteria), antiviral and antifungal. It also stops inflammation in your baby.

There is also an interesting protein called alpha-lactalbumin which protects your baby from malignant tumour cells. The complex is known as HAMLET (human alpha-lactalbumin made lethal to tumour cells). Again, amazing!

We also have carbohydrates in the breast milk. Oligosaccharides go into your baby's large intestine and sweep non beneficial bacteria out from their gut. The carbohydrates also react with helpful bacteria that already exist in the gut, fermenting and forming the baby's own probiotics.

In breastmilk there is a component called IL-7 (Interleukin-7) which contributes towards the production of antibody producing cells as well as having a positive impact on the size of the thymus in the developing baby. The thymus is a gland located between the lungs and it matures cell types known as T-Cells. These T-Cells are vital in the immune response as they recognise and destroy invading unwanted or infected cells.

These are only some examples of the protective components available in breast milk that provide the protection babies need in the early stages of their lives. Until the baby's own immune system matures, the presence of these protective factors allows for the nutritional components present in the milk to go towards the baby's growth and development instead of fighting harmful microbes.

There are many complexities that contribute towards a healthy baby, one who grows up to be active, vibrant, and with a strong immune system. The complexities go beyond what is happening within the mother and the baby. It is understanding the importance of overall health, whether this is the soils our foods are grown in, the air we breathe, or the quality of the water that goes into our food production and into our bodies.

This is important knowledge to have to help keep your baby healthy.

Children's health worldwide has seen an increase in medical conditions such as asthma, autism, allergies, cancers, and auto-immune disorders – conditions that were not often seen only 50 or 60 years ago.

If our focus is on the true power of our body's ability to heal when our systems are in balance, then we can understand that no single man-made medicine can ever replace what a balanced human being's body can achieve, and each and every one of us can contribute to turning this around by making positive choices in daily life. These changes may take many forms, whether it's taking a healthy lunch to work, using non-toxic cleaning products in the home, growing some vegetables in the garden or on a window ledge, or taking a daily walk in nature. There are many changes that can be made, all contributing towards enhancing our own health, as well as that of our families.

There are currently many studies that are helping us to understand the importance of a healthy gut flora (also known as gut microbiome) in everyone's health. Our modern lifestyle, which includes ingesting unhealthy foods and beverages and the overuse of antibiotics, impacts our gut flora.

Health outcomes for a child not being breastfed, or being breastfed for shorter lengths of time, increase the risk of:

∞ Gastrointestinal infections.
∞ Respiratory infections.
∞ Ear infections.
∞ Necrotizing enterocolitis in premature babies.
∞ Dental malocclusions.
∞ Lower intelligence quotient.
∞ Sudden infant death syndrome (SIDS).

Should you be concerned about any of the above conditions please seek assistance from your trusted practitioner.

Developing a Deep Connection with Your Baby

'Mother bonding is
essential for peace'

James W. Prescott

WHEN A WOMAN is pregnant, it is not just nutrients that she is supplying to her baby. Her growing baby is experiencing everything she is seeing and feeling, and consequently, the biology will be adapting to these experiences.

Compare the life of two mothers-to-be. One mother is constantly living in a fearful, unsupported, environment. Her body is in a constant state of survival, being prepared for flight and fight by the release of stress hormones. The other mother lives in a safe, supported environment and she is nurtured by the people around her.

The hormonal signals entering the baby's bloodstream from each mother will have a different effect on the development of her baby. For example, the baby of the woman living in a fearful environment will develop a different brain structure. The area of the brain known as the forebrain (emotions, thinking, evaluating) is suppressed, and the area of the brain known as the hindbrain (the coordinator of functions for survival), is more developed. This prepares the baby for a life of survival which may be needed if the environment they are born into continues to be difficult. The nurturing, compassionate area of the brain is not as developed as it would be for the baby whose mother lives in a supported, nurtured environment. This is natures way of preparing the baby for the particular situation that they will be born into.

The genetics from the parents are involved in the development of the baby in the womb, however, it is the environmental factors that will have the greatest influence on their development.

This is good to know as a woman and her partner may need to make some important decisions before and during the pregnancy.

This may take many forms, from changing food habits, moving house, giving up smoking, adjusting the work environment, learning meditation, fixing negative relationships or singing, talking, and connecting with the baby. With this knowledge, many possibilities are available to influence the creation of a beautiful, calm, creative human being.

When your baby is born, they will have many important moments of imprinting information into their rapidly changing brain. In those first moments following birth, a calm environment with warmth, muted lighting and gentle sounds creates their first experiences of life. This allows a baby to remain calm, adjusting to the new environment.

> *She nestles into a comfortable position on the mother's breast or in the crook of her arm, her head gently relaxed back, enabling her to look up and seek eye to eye contact. The distance from the breast to the mother's face is about 20cm and this is the distance she is able to start focusing on her mother's face which she will be able to see clearly while the surrounding areas will appear blurry. She hears her parent's voices, already familiar to her in the womb, and she is reassured.*

A baby is programmed to identify expressions on the parents' faces, especially their mothers. A smiling, happy face lets them know that the world is fine, however, when a parent's face displays sadness or fear, the baby perceives that something is wrong. When new events occur in a baby's environment, the first thing they do is look for the parent's face. The smiling happy face reassures the baby that everything is okay.

A baby is engaging with their world and learning quickly, and looking up at a parent's face, that is focused on them and present in the moment, is a major part of their development.

In a world where parents are busy with multitudes of things to do, it's easy to become distracted, especially in an age where technologies such as phones, computers, and the television are ever present. A baby looks around for facial contact and when that isn't available to them, they start to focus differently.

In the early days and weeks of their lives, most babies will have an unsettled period within their day or night. Often this time corresponds with the time that they were most active in the womb. If they were quieter during the day, the rocking motion of your walking and moving about had a settling effect on them. In the evening, when you sat down or went to bed, it was time for them to move and wriggle about. This may therefore be the pattern that a baby displays in the early days and months after they are born. This is their time with those who care for them to give them plenty of cuddles, gentle rocking movements, love and reassurance, letting them know that all is well. Your baby, new and vulnerable to the world, relies on you to make them feel safe, secure, and loved.

Conscious Parenting

From conception to six-years of age, the child's brain is mainly working in a subconscious state, shaped by instinct and through the messages received from the environment. Babies are constantly absorbing information from their parents, their surroundings, and others who are in close contact with them.

Around the age of six, they become less susceptible to outside influences. Their conscious mind begins to drive the show. Their learned behaviours and beliefs that were developed from conception to six years of age, is now establishing the future of your child's beliefs and behaviours.

When a parent directs negative statements to their child, e.g., you are not smart or pretty, you lack coordination, you won't amount to much, your child's subconscious mind holds these statements as truth. During early development, your child can't differentiate between a statement said in jest or anger, or what is real or not real. It is best to leave these types of statements out of your daily vocabulary. Think before you speak, especially if you are feeling angry or frustrated. As parents, you have a powerful influence over the development of your child and these statements can live on and effect a child long into their adulthood.

Carrying our Babies

Carrying your young baby close to you is an amazing experience. Your baby will generally be content in the closeness of being with a parent as they will be experiencing the same senses of rhythm, movement, and connection of being in the womb. Babies do not perceive separation from their mother for a period of time. If we compare ourselves with the animal world, newborn animals such horses, cows or elephants are on their feet – often within minutes following birth. Our human babies are dependent upon us for a long time, even the ability to commence walking takes between nine to 14 months.

You may choose to use a baby carrier to carry your baby and keep them close to you. This is reassuring for your baby and lets them know that the world is a safe place for them. It is also important for creating ideal brain development, as movement stimulates the base of the brain, which has major consequences for later brain development.

When using a baby carrier, consider the comfort and position of the baby's body in the carrier. Safely using the carrier is important. Refer to relevant safety guidelines.

Do some research, talk to parents who have used one, and look at reviews on the different products available, to gauge which one will be best for you and your baby. Some considerations:

∞ Choose a carrier that is appropriate for the age and size of your baby.

∞ Find a position where they lie against you in an upright position so that their back is straight.
∞ Allow your baby's face to be side facing, and up close to yours ensuring that their chin is not falling onto their chest. In this position you can observe if they are feeling comfortable and are breathing with a clear space.
∞ Hip comfort is important in a carrier to ensure healthy development of this area. A carrier should support your baby's

thighs well with the hips spread so they are straddling your body and their knees are level or higher than their bottom.

- If you have purchased a carrier, practice using it before you try it out with your baby. Use a small pillow in the carrier and practice the steps of putting it on, so that you can comfortably and easily use it with your baby. Many carrier producers will have a video available which will be helpful.

A well-known developmental psychologist and researcher, James W. Prescott, concluded that hyperexcitability and aggression in adulthood were due to the lack of physical contact and body movement when babies were not held by their mothers, or experienced a lack of social contact with others when they were young. He concluded that a mother's interaction can prevent cycles of violence. Lots of mother–infant interaction and body contact with human touch imprints onto a baby's brain a beautiful, calm connection, minimising their stress and giving them a great start in life.

He studied cultures where parents maintained extensive physical contact with their babies and children and concluded that these were the most peaceful cultures.

Social Expectations

It is an understanding in the modern world that when responding to a baby's needs, holding and carrying them around can be perceived as spoiling them. The ideal baby is seen as the baby who sleeps all night from a very early age, in a cot, in a nursery, in a room away from the parents.

The reality is, babies require their needs to be met well before they show signs of distress. They require regular reassurance and human contact. It is not spoiling them to hold and comfort them in meeting their needs. Their feeding cycles are frequent as their stomachs are small and empty quickly. It takes time for them to develop the regular sleep cycles that we experience as adults. It puts a lot of pressure on parents when they have the expectation that a baby should be sleeping through the night at a particular stage of their early life.

When parents are encouraged to allow their baby to cry it out (leave them to cry until they exhaust themselves and fall asleep) to train the baby to go to sleep at night, they may learn to sleep, but at what cost? How stressful is this on them to go through this? In the process, has the baby learnt to mistrust their world? These are the questions to ask yourself if you are in this situation. Make your decisions on what feels right and comfortable for you as the protector of your baby.

The first twelve months are a vulnerable time for a woman after having a baby. It is wonderful and special for the mother to be with her baby as much as possible, without the pressures and expectations that can be felt to have the perfectly kept house or to always look a certain way.

Be aware of the messages you receive from others in certain situations, such as when your baby is crying.

"You shouldn't be holding her all the time", "you are spoiling her", "you are making a rod for your own back", "maybe you don't provide enough milk, or the quality of milk is no good", "my milk was never enough, maybe yours is the same", or "pass your baby over to me, I can settle her for you".

Even though this help and assistance can be valuable for a new mother, these types of statements can greatly reduce your confidence in your ability to mother your baby.

A simple reply is, "Thank you, I am happy to nurse and care for my baby in this way".

The Power of the Sound

Babies are attuned to their parent's voices. In the womb, a deep connection develops if you take the time to talk, hum, or sing to them. Your baby is feeling the vibrations of the love that you are feeling towards them and this connection with them is very powerful.

Choose gentle or soothing music or sing songs to them that you enjoy. After your baby is born, if they are going through an unsettled period, play the same music or sing these songs and see if this helps bring your baby into a calm and relaxed state. The sound of either parent's calming voice will have a similar effect and helps to develop a deeper connection and reassurance to your baby.

The Power of Human Touch

Our western culture has seen that in previous generations after a baby was born, they often did not experience direct contact with their mother. Immediately following birth, they were wrapped up, placed in a cot, and taken to a nursery. Imagine how the babies must have felt with the lack of human contact, abandoned and in a state of stress, only being brought out to their mothers for scheduled feeding times. What legacy, as they were growing up, did this leave on their feelings of safety, security, and of being valued as a human being? Our understanding of the importance of human contact and loving and nurturing from the start of life has changed from those times. Feeling nurtured and loved is a human right and is essential on our journey through life.

> "Nothing can quite replace the loving touch and nurturing a mother provides for her baby, and through her touch, she nurtures all of humanity. And what about the father? It is the primary role of males to protect and support the women they love, so they can nurture all our children."
>
> James W. Prescott.

If a baby is born unwell or premature and requires assistance in breathing, recent studies indicate that early resuscitation is possible and can be beneficial with the baby and mother together. The baby, still attached to the pulsating cord is receiving vital extra oxygen, iron, and stem cells.

These babies may require extra care in a Special Care Unit (SCU). The importance of a mother's contact is especially important in these circumstances. Reclining chairs placed next to a humidicrib allows parents to spend as much time as possible once the baby's condition is stable. Long hours of skin-to-skin contact, also known as kangaroo care with the mother or father is encouraged.

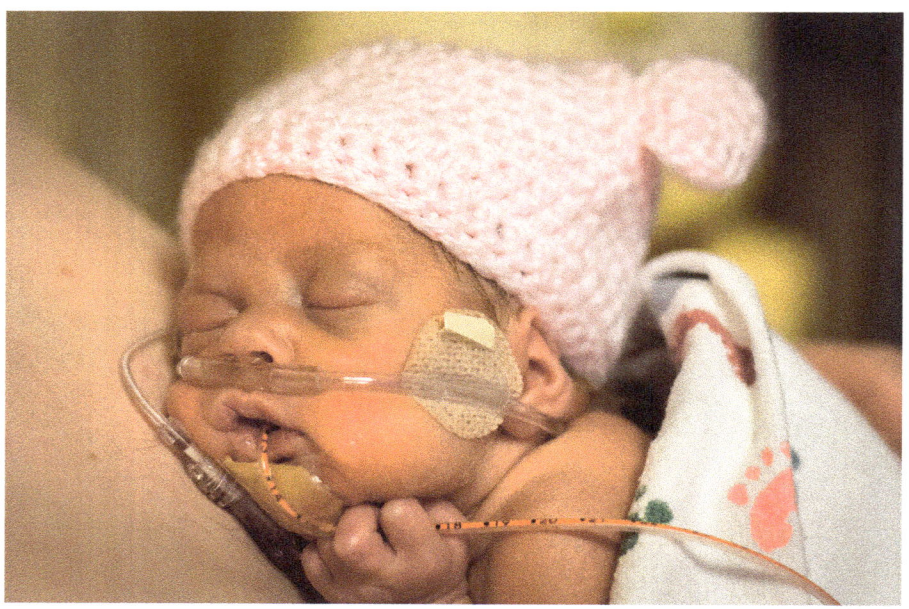

TIP

 A little exercise I do with new parents is to get them to think of themselves as a newborn baby. We were all newborns once, however, we have no conscious memory of that time.

What would it feel like, if the first thing you experience is being placed on your mother's stomach? What would the noises around you be? How would you feel if the noises were really loud? What if you were taken off you mother's warm chest and placed on cold scales with bright lights? How would you feel if everyone around you is talking in loud voices? How can you help them realise how vulnerable and sensitive you are right now? What if the environment was too cold? What if there were lots of funny chemical smells around from deodorants, perfumes and disinfectants? How would that feel to your senses?

What if you were home with your mother and you had a pain in your stomach and needed comforting. You are crying, but your mother had been told that if she picks you up, she would be spoiling you. You are distressed. You fall asleep out of exhaustion. How are you feeling about the world when you wake up?

Babies are vulnerable beings and cannot fend for themselves. We would have a different world if our understanding of babies and human connection were different.

Your Sleeping Baby

NEWBORN BABIES HAVE a need to sleep a lot in the early months of their lives. Often, their sleep/wake cycles reflect the rhythm they developed while they were in the womb. Now in your arms, these rhythms are embedded into their system, so if you observe this in your baby, understand and work with this knowledge. If your baby sleeps deeper and longer in the daytime, which most babies do in the early weeks, allow this to happen. Take a rest yourself when your baby is sleeping. You will be better able to cope in the times when they are more restless, which often occurs later in the evening or into the night. As babies get older, they become more attuned to the difference between day and night. This internal body clock of sleep/wake cycles is known as a circadian rhythm and there are different things you can do to help your baby establish these sleep cycles.

When you are pregnant, maintain a regular eating and sleeping schedule for yourself, as this enables your growing baby to pick up on your cycles through hormonal exchange and your daily movements. If you are eating on the run, having irregular sleep times, including lots of late nights, this may not be beneficial to establishing your baby's sleep/wake cycles after they are born.

Once your baby is born, ensure that they are sleeping in close proximity to you as it has been shown that a baby and their mother are attuned to each other's sleeping cycles. If, for example, you are both in a light sleep cycle, responding to feeding and settling and going back to sleep will be much quicker and easier. It also gives them a deeper sense of security to be near you. Babies have a survival instinct, and when feeling secure in their world, will more easily drift back to sleep.

If they have been too disturbed in the night, releasing lots of the stress hormones, this reduces the amount of melatonin (sleep inducing hormone) that they receive. Getting back to sleep will be more difficult for both of you.

Make day and night different from the beginning. In the daytime hours, have your baby in the room where there is everyday activity. Your baby will be accustomed to the normal noises of the household. Have the room well-lit by the natural daylight. A pleasant walk or spending some time outside would be great if possible. In the evening, once the sun goes down, turn the lighting levels low. Limiting exposure to artificial light after sunset helps towards your baby developing their wake/sleep cycles. Studies show that the blue light from the technology we use (TVs, computers, and phones) as well as the light from LED bulbs, suppress or delay the release of melatonin. This is the time when noise levels are quieter and the atmosphere in the house is more relaxed. This becomes the settling down phase in their daily rhythm.

It is perfectly normal for a baby to get sleepy or fall asleep at the breast as breast milk contains hormones which will make you and your baby relaxed and sleepy:
- ∞ Oxytocin, the hormone of love.
- ∞ Endorphins, the hormones of pleasure.
- ∞ Prolactin, the hormones of mothering.
- ∞ CCK (cholecystokinin) is released into the baby's gut when they start sucking, making them feel full and sleepy.
- ∞ Hormone levels of melatonin are high in breast milk at night.

STORY

I remember a woman I was caring for was waking her two-day old baby up after it had just completed a feed.

I asked her why she was waking him up as he was sleeping peacefully.

She said that she had been told that she was spoiling her baby and that he wouldn't learn to go to sleep by himself if she let him drift off to sleep on the breast while feeding.

I gently explained some of the processes that were occurring when her newborn fed. I explained to her that breast milk has different components in it that makes them sleepy. The amounts of these components increase in the evening and night time, making them even sleepier.

Giving her this understanding of what was normal for a newborn helped her to understand that falling asleep at the breast was what nature intended.

I explained to her that breast milk has different components in it that makes them sleepy. The amounts of these components increase in the evening and night-time, making them even sleepier.

TIP

If there is a time when your baby is unable to directly breastfeed and is receiving expressed breast milk instead, make sure that the milk they receive at night has been expressed at night.

Developing good ways of managing your life in these early months can have positive benefits for healthy sleeping habits. It may take several months for your baby's system to regulate their sleep/wake cycles. Around three months of age, a baby's own melatonin production increases significantly.

TIP

Some parents have the belief that their baby must be in a darkened, quiet room during the day to assist them to sleep. This can create difficulties when you start to go out and about, as your baby may find it difficult to sleep anywhere other than in a quiet dark space.

As your baby gets older and feels safe and content in their world, they will begin to settle themselves when they are still awake, relaxed, and sleepy.

A well nurtured baby will learn to self soothe

TIPS

The advice to feed your baby more often in the day so that they sleep longer at night may sound good in theory, however, remember that babies, like adults, enjoy and digest food better when feeling hungry. Waking your baby to feed in this situation may cause them to be sleepy in their effort to feed, to only take a partial feed, or take in the milk before the previous feed has been digested. If these habits persist into childhood and adulthood, they can contribute to overeating and digestive upsets. Babies do not know about clocks, only their own natural rhythms and needs.

- Just before the feed is finishing, dressing your baby into heavier or specific night wear, or doing a final nappy change if required, creates minimal disturbance and should be easier for them to remain asleep and settled as you move them into their sleeping area. If you dress them in a heavier night outfit too early during the feed, they may become too hot.

- When a baby falls asleep at the breast at the end of a feed, initially they will be in a lighter pattern of sleep, therefore more easily disturbed. If they are waking when you are putting them down into their sleeping area, it is worth waiting longer (approximately 20–25 minutes), as this is when they drift into a deeper level of sleep.

- Be aware of social pressures. It is often inferred, either indirectly or directly, that a baby sleeping through the night is a good baby. This may make you feel like you are failing in your role as a mother if this is not happening, or you may feel pressured to try and make this happen before your baby is ready.

- Creating a sleep trigger will be helpful in settling your baby. A baby will learn to associate an action with going to sleep if the action is done on a regular basis. This may be as simple as dressing your baby in a certain type of outfit prior to sleep, for example, a zip up baby sleeping bag. This is especially helpful for the older baby as they are often awake after a feed. When they start to show their tired signs, such as becoming restless, pulling at their ear, or stretching their body, getting them dressed in their particular sleep outfit will help them understand and welcome sleep. A warm evening bath can also be a trigger for sleep as well as being relaxing.

I will leave you with this quote:

> *"This combination of nature and nurture will be enhanced when we follow our babies' cues, which tell us about their developmental needs at every stage of parenting. It can be reassuring to know that we don't need a degree in child development to mother well, only the willingness to respond to our instincts and our babies, in a way that brings peace, joy, and ease at each age and stage."*
>
> Sarah J. Buckley, MD

The Sleeping Space

When preparing for the arrival of your baby, one of the decisions that you will need to look at is where your baby will be sleeping. Understanding the needs of the baby is important as they have an ongoing need to feel secure and being reassured through close contact. Some form of co-sleeping is recommended. Co-sleeping is defined as being close to, but not necessarily sharing, the same bed surface with a parent, usually the mother. This is where you are able to see, hear, touch, and smell your baby, or in other words, you are in arms reach of your baby.

When in close proximity, the regular breathing of the mother (or parent) regulates the baby's breathing. Synchronised breathing patterns allows for better sleep. The baby also spends less time in deep sleep allowing themselves to be easily aroused if their oxygen levels decrease.

Finding out information on possible safe sleeping arrangements before your baby arrives will help you to decide what will be the best options for where your baby will sleep. I have listed safe sleeping guidelines in the resources section of this book, and they are important guidelines to understand as each family's situation is unique.

Sleep Deprivation for the Parents and How to Manage

It is interesting that when parents or parents-to-be, discuss the experience of having a baby, one of the main concerns is coping with sleep deprivation. Remember the nights when you were younger and out and about with friends well into the night, and how you felt the next day. Sleep deprivation is not the most pleasant of experiences. Your energy and motivation are at a low.

A woman through the latter stages of her pregnancy has her system primed for changes in sleep patterns. The need for getting up frequently to pass urine as the baby descends deeper into the pelvis, or feeling uncomfortable and restless as she finds a more comfortable position in bed, can be challenging.

These disturbances are something that you become somewhat accustomed to, switching off and back to sleep once the cause of the disturbance is resolved.

When your baby arrives in your life, the following tips may help you get the maximum sleep possible:

- Feed your baby in low level lighting as bright lights and any unnecessary noise will make it more difficult for both of you to get back to sleep.
- Ensure your baby gets a full feed in the night, not just a quick snack. The longer feed will ensure the baby gets the fatty milk which comes as the breast is emptying. This will be more satisfying for them.
- If the previous feed was a short time before, it may be unnecessary to change the nappy, creating less disturbance for the baby and therefore allowing the baby to drift back to sleep more easily.
- If you are unable to directly breastfeed your baby and expressing/bottling instead, make sure the baby gets milk that is expressed in the night as it is higher in the sleepy hormones.
- In the early weeks and months, taking one or two daily naps will make all the difference to the night feeding experience, especially if your baby is having an unsettled night.
- Your partner, or enlisting helpful parents or other family members to assist at night with burping, nappy changing and settling, can be a big help in the early weeks.
- If you are up in the night and you are feeling hungry, avoid eating a heavy snack, as this will make getting back to sleep difficult. A small piece of fruit maybe sufficient.
- Stocking up the freezer with meals or asking family/friends to help with some meals can make a big difference to getting more daytime rest. Make sure the meals have ingredients in them that are what you normally eat otherwise your baby may become unsettled from the changes.

∞ If you do experience the feeling of tiredness during the day, instead of saying to yourself or others, *I am so tired*, repeat the words, *I feel refreshed and energetic*, even if it does not feel true. The positive messages will become ingrained into your subconscious and make a big difference to how you are feeling.

∞ Feeding your baby at night does not last forever! Even though it may not feel like it at the time, these experiences are very special moments. Embrace them. Your baby grows up very fast.

∞ Recognise if things become too much for you as we are all different. Reach out for help if you need it.

The Unsettled Baby

MOST BABIES HAVE an unsettled period within their day or night. This unsettled period is common and normal and generally requires lots of cuddles and support for your baby to allow them to feel safe and secure in their world.

Some babies, however, may never look settled or comfortable in their bodies from the very beginning of their life, or they have extremely long periods of crying and being unsettled. Working out what might be considered normal and what is not can be difficult, especially if this is your first experience of being a mother.

If you feel there are any underlying issues, it is important to get your baby's health checked by a doctor who specialises in baby care (paediatrician).

If there are no underlying health issues, make some observations around what is happening in the daily life of your baby. Recording this information in a journal will be helpful for you to work out what is going on and recognise patterns of behaviour. It will also be helpful information to have with you if you do need to go and visit a health practitioner.

Ask yourself, and record in the journal, answers to questions such as:

- What time of the day or night is your baby most unsettled?
- Do their unsettled periods occur before or after feeds?
- Is your baby having adequate wet and dirty nappies?
- What is the colour, quantity, odour of your baby's urine and bowel motions?
- Is your baby having adequate weight gains?
- What length of time is your baby unsettled for?
- Does your baby look bright and alert when they are awake?
- Is your baby well attached onto the breast? Is there any pain, clicking or slurping sounds when your baby is feeding? Are the nipples misshaped immediately after a feed indicating poor attachment?
- Prior to the unsettled periods, did you have any food or beverages that you normally wouldn't consume?
- Is your baby scheduled (by the clock) or demand fed?
- Is your baby receiving anything else other than breast milk? If so, record what your baby is being given, including any medications and wind drops.

A baby becomes attuned to your particular food intake while you are pregnant through the ingestion of amniotic fluid and blood flow. If eating habits after your baby is born remain fairly consistent (assuming that the eating habits are healthy), then usually the food that you eat will not create a problem for the breastfeeding baby.

If your baby is experiencing a prolonged unsettled period with crying, drawing up their legs, and looking uncomfortable in the body and they are normally calm and settled most of the time, then take a look back over the previous 24 hours. You may be able to identify something that contributed to this episode. The culprit may be as simple as having eaten some food that is different from what you would normally eat. For example, remembering that your auntie brought over a casserole you found rich. It contained items that you normally didn't eat, and you noticed your baby became very unsettled sometime after eating the meal.

For the baby who is continually unsettled, look at the items of food you are eating that are considered common allergens. Intact proteins can cross into your breast milk. Examples of common foods that can create problems for babies are cow's milk protein, eggs, soy, or wheat. It is easy to eliminate these items for several weeks, starting with one item at a time to see if there is any difference in your baby's behaviour. Record your findings in a journal to get an accurate picture of any results. When eliminating food items, ensure that you are replacing those foods with other items so you don't become deficient in vitamins or minerals. Chewing food well, eating in a relaxed atmosphere with few distractions, and taking the time to enjoy your food will help improve the absorption and balance in your system. A visit to a nutritionist or dietician may help you as well.

If the unsettled periods for your baby are occurring in the evening or overnight, take note of where you are settling your baby. If settling time is in front of a large television or computer screen, this may be having a negative effect. There is an electronic field around these devices, and babies can be sensitive to this as well as the blue light that is emitted which suppresses or delays the release of the sleep hormone melatonin.

TIP

 Move your baby's sleeping area to a different area within the room they normally sleep or in a different part of the house.

Problems can arise if your baby is sleeping in close proximity to products which are outside the house, such as meter boxes, or devices that measure power usage. Consider turning off internet modems when not in use at night as this may be helpful. There are products designed to reduce the effects of electronic fields, and researching this subject is worthwhile.

Observing your baby's bowel actions can help determine if there are any imbalances in their system. When breastfeeding, I encourage the full 'emptying' of a breast prior to changing to the other side, if the other side is required. Timing the length of time on each breast may result in partial emptying of the breasts, resulting in a baby having access to large quantities of low-fat breast milk. This can be especially evident in women with large breast milk storage capacity. Lactose requires enzyme activity to break it down into a digestible form. Large amounts of low-fat breast milk move quickly down the baby's digestive system, resulting in the amount of the enzyme available in the baby's gut becoming insufficient for the large amount of lactose. The bowel action in this situation becomes loose, watery, or green, often resulting in an unsettled baby who is crying, uncomfortable, and sucking on the fists for comfort.

A mother or baby who has received a course of antibiotics can become unsettled with changes to the bowel actions as the gut flora has become unbalanced.

Incorrect attachment onto the breast can also contribute towards a baby becoming unsettled. When a baby has a shallow attachment, she will tend to come on and off the breast in the effort to find a deeper attachment. She will use up a lot more energy in the process, especially if she is upset and crying in her efforts. Smaller amounts of milk will be releasing to her as she feeds. She is working harder and staying on the breast longer (or giving up) in an effort to get what she needs. Some babies become too exhausted and fall asleep before their hunger is fully satisfied, resulting in shorter sleeps before hunger wakes them up again.

A good seal around the baby's mouth when they are on the breast is required to prevent excessive wind. When a baby is not attaching well, or the physical structure of the mouth, lips and tongue area does not allow a complete seal, excessive air is ingested into the stomach. Excessive wind causes discomfort. When a baby is in pain, they look for comfort by sucking on their hands. This can often be interpreted as hunger and the baby re-fed. If the milk from the previous feed has not digested properly, a cycle of discomfort occurs.

TIP

 If a baby is in pain, their body will look uncomfortable. They will draw their legs up to their chest and move around a lot, as well as sucking vigorously on their fists. A baby who is hungry will be sucking on their fist and moving their head towards the breast but will look comfortable in their body. This can be confusing at first, however, you will soon learn to recognise the difference.

All babies experience some build-up of air in their stomachs and opportunities to allow the release of air from your baby's system throughout the feed is required for comfort. Your baby will often indicate when it is time to be burped by becoming restless. When it is time, sit your baby up in a supported position on your lap or place her onto your chest supporting her body with your hands with gentle tapping and movements. Babies can find relief by releasing built up air from both ends.

TIP

 Babies who bring up their milk regularly will require this transition into the sitting burping position to be done slowly.

Another reason your baby may be unsettled is if they are too hot or cold. If their body temperature is not right, they may find it difficult to settle. I know as an adult it can be hard to get a restful night's sleep if I am too hot or cold.

Many babies find the transition into life, away from the comfort of being in the watery environment of uterine life, difficult. Here they experienced a constant temperature, internal noises, gently rocking when their mother moved, floating in freedom, unencumbered by layers of clothing. It should be no surprise that their favourite place to settle is on the chests of their parents where they are warm, supported, and can hear the noises they were used to.

Reflux

Reflux refers to the contents of the stomach coming back up into the oesophagus (food tube from the back of the throat to the stomach). The milk that has been in a stomach has been in an acid solution. This acid is there to break the milk down so it can be absorbed into the body. Reflux can show up as anything from a little milk dribbling out of the mouth during or after the feed (sometimes hours after a feed) to a more forceful or projectile vomiting. There can be many reasons some babies bring up milk. This can range from trapped air, feeding problems, or an immature digestive system.

Most babies are happy and relaxed about bringing up some milk, as releasing air that comes up with the milk gives them relief.

For some babies, however, pain can be experienced with reflux. This pain can range from mild to more extreme.

At the lower end of the oesophagus, there is a ring of muscles whose job it is to keep the milk down in the stomach. These muscles in a baby have periods of relaxation, especially in the younger baby, allowing the release of trapped air, making them feel more comfortable. It is not until three weeks of age and onwards that these muscles start to exert more pressure. Problems may arise if there is weakness in this muscle's sphincter.

A baby's stomach moves and squeezes food further down the digestive system, however, a baby's gut is sluggish. The emptying time of the baby's stomach contributing to reflux, may become painful.

Feeding problems also have a place in the reflux story, from taking in milk too quickly, to structural issues in a baby's mouth, such as a high palate (roof of the mouth) or a tongue tie (a tight piece of tissue under the tongue that stops the tongue from lifting sufficiently). A seal is created around the breast when a baby is well attached, and structural challenges can prevent this from happening. An incomplete seal allows the entry of excessive air into their gut.

When a baby has reflux, sleep disturbances can be present. When a baby is placed in the sleep position on her back, milk bubbles up. The milk which has been bathed in the stomach acid comes up, causing the oesophagus and throat area to become irritated, waking the baby up with a sudden episode of pain. If the throat area is irritated from the gastric juices in this area, the baby's body will manufacture excessive mucous, which will make them sound congested or noisy in their breathing.

When a baby is feeding and experiences reflux, swallowing can become painful, with the baby pulling away. Being hungry and wanting to feed again, creating a cycle of on and off feeding that contributes to more air intake, which worsens the problem. These babies are fussy and fidgety while feeding, with many pulling away and arching their backs with a scream-like cry. In this situation, a baby can use up a lot of energy, and some babies over a period of time, can experience slow weight gains.

Some babies have what is known as silent reflux which shows up with difficulties in their feeding, or painful episodes as described above, however, the milk does not come up into the baby's mouth or beyond. The milk, mixed with the stomach acid, creates the irritation as it is coming up into the oesophagus only.

STORY

Recently I had a visit from a woman with the most delightful two and half month-old baby. This normally placid and happy baby was having periods of inconsolable crying. I worked through all the possible causes with the mother.

When I asked about how often she fed her baby, she told me that she was feeding her baby every three hours during the day. I asked her if her baby was indicating wanting to be fed at these times. She then said that her baby didn't always look hungry when she woke from her sleep, but she fed her anyway, as recently she had been given the advice that if she fed her baby more frequently in the daytime this would encourage her to sleep for longer periods at night. I suggested that feeding her baby at clock intervals instead of waiting till she indicated the need for a feed, was probably causing the problem. Her baby may not have fully digested the previous feed when being offered another one.

I explained that babies, just like adults experience digestive upsets (pain, excessive gas, stomach cramps) when tempted to overeat, eat when not feeling hungry or eat too quickly.

On following the advice to only feed her baby on demand, this mother contacted me the following week and said that the periods of inconsolable crying and being in pain had stopped, and her baby was back to her settled and delightful self.

Understanding reflux and some helpful techniques can improve the situation, as reflux can be distressing. This can include frequent burping of your baby when your baby indicates she needs to be burped and offering the feed only when she is hungry and not by the timing feeds (i.e., demand feeding, unless the baby is experiencing poor weight gains). Slow, gentle handling of the baby will allow the milk to settle into her stomach as well as allowing plenty of time with her held in an upright position before she is placed in a horizontal sleeping position.

As a baby is unable to talk, their cry is their way of communicating with us. Working with a baby with reflux can be challenging if they are crying for long periods of time. Support from family and friends who are willing to help can be invaluable.

A visit to a paediatrician will be needed if reflux begins to have any effect on the baby's general wellbeing, to check for any underlying health conditions.

Emotional Health

OVER THE YEARS of working as a midwife, I started to notice a trend in how many women had medical histories which included some form of mental illness such as anxiety or depression, either currently or in the past. I started to question what was going on here and why I had not noticed this earlier on in my career. I questioned whether it was because previously, mental health held a stigma around it and subsequently was not discussed as openly as it is now, or if mental illness was increasing.

At a recent conference I attended, the lecturer stated that suicide was a leading cause of death for women in the period after birth. This was very concerning to me. Being aware and understanding how to make positive changes towards our mental health is important. The following information is offered as general health information. Please seek professional guidance when needed.

Overall Health, a Good Place to Start

Changes in the chemistry in your body can affect your emotional health. If your body is in balance and you are experiencing vitality, you will feel much more ready and able to face any challenges that come into your life.

If you are eating foods that are highly processed, lacking essential vitamins and minerals, eating on the run, or living in a constant stressed state, your body will feel this disrespect, your vitality will drain away, and your emotional health will suffer. At the same time, if you are suppressing emotions or negative feelings about yourself with alcohol, drugs, or the overuse of pharmaceutical medication, your body chemistry changes will leave you feeling tired and worn out. Interrupted or poor sleeping habits can also have a negative impact.

Take a conscious look at all aspects of your life. Leading up to making a choice to bring a baby into your world would be a perfect time to consider making these changes. Making changes can create challenges, as the habits we develop throughout our lives have been programed into us and can be difficult to shift. Understanding this, and how the mind works, can help towards making long lasting positive changes to our mental health.

The mind has two parts – the conscious mind and the subconscious mind. The conscious mind holds our positive thoughts; it is the creative part of our brain that holds our desires and aspirations. Our subconscious mind is habitual by nature and is shaped by instinct and the messages it receives from the environment we live in.

The two parts of the mind are interlinked, and most of the time it is the subconscious mind that is in control. Making changes in your life may not be as simple as deciding to make those changes. An example might be deciding (conscious mind) that are you going to start eating healthy foods and exercising daily in an endeavour to feel more vitality and energy, however, your subconscious mind likes things as they are (habits). A conflict between the two parts of the mind begins (conflicting realities). With both parts of the mind sending out different messages, a conflict is created within the mind and self-sabotage occurs.

Unfortunately, using willpower to change these programmes may not work. For example, have you experienced times in your life when you decided that you were going to eat only healthy foods, finding that when presented with something sweet and unhealthy, justifying to yourself, "I deserve a treat", eating it and then feeling bad afterwards? Maybe you were told as a child if you were good and ate all your vegetables, you could have a sweet treat. A subconscious programme was being created – only if I am good will I be rewarded.

Most of these programmes were created in the early phase of our childhood (conception to six years of age) when our brain function was in a subconscious state. In this state, the brain was absorbing all the information it was receiving about the environment that you were growing up in. As we grew older, our brains begin to work on a conscious level as well. Once we understand how our brain works and how this effects our daily living it is also important to know that most of the programming that is non beneficial to us can be reprogrammed in a positive and beneficial way with different therapies. Below is my story of how a modality called Emotional Freedom Techniques (EFT) came into my life and how it assisted me.

STORY

When I was travelling overseas many years ago, I met an interesting woman called Jenny. She introduced me to E.F.T., Emotional Freedom Technique. These techniques induce relaxation using tapping points on the body, also known as acupressure. This rapidly reduces the fight and flight response, reducing the stress hormones in our bodies and balancing the body's energy system.

When I returned home, I started to study E.F.T with Jenny, who is an E.F.T trainer, and completed my practitioner course.

As I continued through the course, I saw more and more changes occurring in my life. I increased my self-confidence and self-worth, as well as changed behaviours and patterns that were not helpful to my life.

I had always wondered why in the evenings I had this desire to eat toast, butter, and honey. Through E.F.T. I discovered that as a student nurse at a major city hospital, after a busy and often challenging day, I would go back to the nurse's home where they supplied thick toast, butter and honey.

I would sit together with some of my colleagues to discuss the challenges we faced. It was a comforting and supportive time of the day. Once I discovered the association of comfort and eating toast, I used E.F.T. and found the craving for the toast melted away.

Other results of using E.F.T was discovering the reason I felt uncomfortable as an adult in a setting where the focus

> was on me. The realisation was, I had been brought up in an environment where children were seen but not heard, especially in social settings. These feelings of low self-worth and lack of confidence melted away after working with E.F.T.
>
> The beauty of doing this course was that there was plenty of practise, working on myself, either by myself or with other EFT students.

Put downs and labelling you received as a child by parents, family, or community members such as teachers, can have long lasting effects on your emotional health. You may not even be aware of the effects these statements have had on your life. Working through the areas of your emotional health with modalities such as E.F.T will help bring some of these labels or putdowns to the surface, in order for you to clear them, and if done effectively, these changes are permanent.

Another helpful technique that I have found to be beneficial is the use of affirmations. Affirmations work by convincing the subconscious mind that something is true by repetition. The affirmation statement that you make is made as if it's happening right now in this moment. For example, if you are lacking confidence in your ability to mother your baby, repeating out loud "I am confident in my ability to look after my baby". Whatever statement you choose to make, write it on a note and put it in different places around the house so that you see it and repeat it often. You will be surprised how changes will occur in how you feel. I have included some affirmations in the reference section of this book that you may like to use if they resonate with you.

The beauty of working with techniques such as affirmations or modalities such as E.F.T. is that they can be used as self-help techniques. Empowering yourself is important, however, my recommendation is that if you have experienced any deep trauma, whatever modality is suitable for you, find a trusted practitioner to work with. Deeper experiences of trauma come with many layers to be worked through. Remember if you are ever tempted into trying to change the behaviour of others around you, this generally does not work, however, by working on yourself, watch magic happen to the behaviour of those around you.

Becoming a parent is a good time to question what you want in life. Where you want to live, who you want to be around, and how you want to live. Where is the fun in your life? What is creating drudgery in your life? Above all, what gives you joy? If you make changes and good choices in your life, your emotional health and well-being will improve immensely.

By working to release old beliefs/patterns and increasing your self-worth, you can move from thinking in survival mode to an empowered state. It is from this state that you can mould your new way of being. If your emotional health is below par, that is what your baby will mirror.

When you are healthy emotionally, this will flow easily and effortlessly to your child. By modelling self-care and honouring yourself, you are the best example for your child and those around you.

A Commitment to Parenting

THIS CHAPTER IS written to encourage you and your partner to consciously think about how you both can work together to create a happy, healthy, and peaceful way of living and responding to your baby's needs as they grow.

Below is a list of possible ideas that you might like to start with. Add your own ideas as well and remove the ones that don't resonate with you. When you have created your own list, print it out and refer back to it regularly.

1. I wish to teach my baby (and myself) to embrace the joy of living in the moment. I will spend time with my baby and enjoy her company. I will manage the use of electronic devices such as mobile phones, so I am not distracted in these precious moments. When I'm sitting with my baby and she is looking up at me, I will look back at her, hold her close and embrace the moment.

2. I will work hard to provide comfort, shelter, and security for my baby, without the burden and feeling the pressures of wanting bigger and better things which would keep me

working longer and harder than necessary. My child wants my time, not things.

3. I will encourage my baby to learn at her own comfortable rate of learning. I will not put pressure on my baby to meet everyone else's expectations.
4. I will treat my baby as an individual who has her own way of expressing herself in this world. I won't be caught up in comparing her with others.
5. I will be aware of what I am saying when my baby and I are in the presence of others. I will be mindful not to have conversations that are constantly negative or about negative topics. I will endeavour to leave a conversation with people feeling brighter and inspired by my positivity. Constant negative talk can become a habit. I will be aware of my conversations.
6. I will not put labels on my baby, and I will discourage others from doing this as well. By repeating limited descriptors often enough, such as, "she looks just like her auntie who wasn't very smart", or "he has the same build as his cousin who was always very clumsy", this can become part of their limiting belief system.
7. I will develop an attitude of wellness. I will demonstrate how powerful my body is when given the right environment to stay healthy and heal. I will take on the responsibility of my own health and I will role model this to my baby.
8. I will create a peaceful environment for my baby and I will deal with life challenges in a peaceful manner. If my partner and I are feeling under pressure, or a conflict of ideas arises,

we will agree to only deal with these issues away from the presence of our baby.

9. I will teach my baby good food habits as she grows.
10. I will model laughter, fun, play, and enjoyment of life and an attitude of relaxation. I will be aware of the need to continually strive for things in my life.

Assisting the Environment

WHAT SORT OF environmental legacy do you want to leave your children? Being ecofriendly and assisting the environment is a mindset. It's about asking questions and making positive changes in your life.

Parenting transforms your thinking. Now you have a child or are about to have one, I am sure you want your world to be greener and cleaner in a healthier way.

Your Home

Let's start with your home for a cleaner, greener environment. This is the place that your baby comes home to, so it's important to take a good look around and sort it out, preferably before they arrive.

Developing an appreciation for your home environment and creating good habits around the things you do and the products you purchase, will assist the environment well into the future.

Expensive chemical laden products have only been around for a short time. When I was growing up, cleaning a bench top meant wiping it down with a cloth and water and a little soap. Now, we are encouraged to spray manufactured products around to clean. Then, when the bottle is empty, it is thrown away to land fill.

> **TIP**
>
> Wipe benches with a reusable cloth and water. If the bench is greasy, consider changes you can make to the way you prepare your food, avoiding oils and grease. To clean grease, use a bit of soap in the cloth, then wipe. For more stubborn stains I use a product that is natural and non-toxic (Gumption paste), and a cheap and long-lasting alternative to the modern cleaning products on the shelves. It is useful when needing to clean any residue or grease from the kitchen, bathrooms, showers, baths, sinks and ovens (always do a small test with any product).

If you like to have a pleasant and clean smell around after you have cleaned, use a few drops of plant-derived aromatherapy oil such as eucalyptus or lemongrass in your paste. Make sure you purchase quality aromatherapy oils and not the synthetic version called fragrant oils, which are toxic.

For your laundry powder, use one that is biodegradable and doesn't contain phosphates. Choose one that is made in Australia and comes in a cardboard box instead of plastic (for effective disposal of the container.) When I was researching information, I came across a product called soap berries. These berries come from a tree and create a soap effect. According to the reviews, they work very effectively. Baking soda or white vinegar can be used as a stain remover and fabric softener. Not only will your home and clothes be naturally clean and nontoxic, but it will also save you a great amount of money. One particular brand of washing powder is now packaging their product without a plastic scoop, to assist the environment.

If you have a great idea, such as a change to a product's packaging, why not contact the manufacturers of the product and suggest your idea.

> **TIP**
>
> Think about clearing out other toxic products from your house and shed while you are at it. For example, herbicides, pesticides, and insect sprays. Look for effective replacements. Weeds can be pulled out by hand, or you can pour boiling water on them. Insect sprays can be made using aromatherapy oils such as lemongrass, lavender oil, tea tree and geranium.

Shopping

Another product that I came across in my research was a set of bags for storing fruits and vegetables in the fridge. The reusable bags maintain an environment where the produce keeps fresh for a longer period time, therefore less waste and no plastic bags. (Reference: The Swag Bag).

I use another product that you take to the shops along with your reusable shopping bags. They are little net bags with a drawer string that you place the fruit and vegetables in (no plastics bags needed).

In our community, the supermarkets are not supplying the plastic bags for grocery items. These need to be purchased. Hopefully, consumers will remember to bring in their bags each time they shop. These plastic bags which are still for sale, are potentially not going to last as long as the others and they still need to be disposed of. I've had some of my shopping bags for years, and store these in the car boot as I try to do a visit to the shops on my way home, as I go past the shops, avoiding extra trips in the car. I also buy smaller amounts of food more frequently. This saves a lot of food needing to be thrown away. It means that your food has more nutritional value because it is as fresh as possible.

When purchasing your fresh produce, be mindful to choose products that have little or no wrapping around them. Choose fruit and vegetables that are not pre-packaged. They are cheaper and have less impact on landfill. All vegetable scraps can be composted and returned to your garden, ensuring even less waste. For people in small homes or apartments, there are suitable products to assist with composting. Have a look around your home and see how you can contribute to assisting the environment more.

Setting Up a Room For Your Baby

Ideally a baby's room is used for storing bits and pieces that your baby will require and not as a sleeping area. It is recommended that a baby sleeps in close proximity to you, as a parent.

If you plan to paint and decorate your baby's room, consider paint products that have zero volatile organic compounds

(VOC) in them. VOC's are gases that are emitted into the air from products or processes and can be harmful to your overall health. If you are pregnant, consider having someone else to do the painting.

Look into the type of floor coverings that may be the healthiest and environmentally friendly. For example, carpet may harbour toxins from the manufacturing process and in the long term, harbour moulds or dust mites. Floor rugs, (organic wool or cotton) if needed on a hard wood, maybe a better alternative, as they should be easier to clean and they can be aired outside when the weather is suitable.

If laying flooring, things to consider:

- ∞ Source of material. Are precious rainforests being cut down in the manufacturing process or are the products sourced from sustainable resources? Are the products coming from local or overseas markets? Consider the transport kilometres it takes to get that product to you.
- ∞ How long will the flooring last? Cheap flooring wears out quickly, it cannot be re-sanded and is designed to be thrown away when showing wear and tear, adding to the destructive landfill.
- ∞ Know what chemicals are involved in the manufacturing, or used on the flooring once it is laid (hard wood floors can be coated with non-toxic polish or safe oils).

Baby Furniture

Baby furniture may be sourced as second-hand furniture (ensure that they meet your countries safety guidelines). This is a good environmental and money saving option. If you paint or decorate any of the furniture, make sure it is the zero VOC paint, and allow plenty of time for the pieces to settle and air before your baby uses them.

Spend the money and time to research for a good quality mattress. The mattress should fit snuggly into the cot with no gaps around it. Check that it is made from non-toxic materials such as organic cottons (foam mattresses are treated with fire retardants).

There are a lot more safe, comfortable, breathable mattress options out there than were available in the past, so do your research and spend the money on this important item.

Sheets and blankets should also be sourced from organic cotton or wool. Wash them well before using them to rid them of any dust or chemicals used in manufacturing.

The Nappy Revolution

You have lots of choices to make when you become pregnant and are planning to bring a new life into your home. One of the most obvious ones is the type of nappy you will choose for your baby. A newborn baby may need to be changed 8 to 12 times a day – that's a lot of nappies. For most people, this choice stops at the brand of disposables on the market and never consider the alternative of cloth nappies. Why? Maybe it is the perception that they take a lot of time and effort to use, or that they are bulky or costly.

If you are using full cloth nappies with a liner and cover system , you only need to wash every second day. Cloth nappy care involves a dry bucket system, where the soiled nappies are placed in a bucket with the lid on and on alternate days the nappies from the bucket are placed into the washing machine, washed, and then hung out to dry. This does not take much effort once you are set up and organised.

The range of cloth nappies on the market now are so much more efficient and easier to use, compared with the cloth ones I used for my children when they were babies. The development of new materials means they are a lot less bulky than they were previously and they now come in some bright, fun colours and patterns. They are also wonderfully comfortable for your baby to wear. They are not hard to care for at all if you consider that the washing machine does most of the work for you.

In our summers, with lots of sunshine, the nappies benefit from being dried in the sun, disinfecting and removing any stains naturally.

In the colder months placing them on a portable clothes airer is easy and reduces your household bills and takes away the environmental impact of using electric clothes dryers.

Cloth nappies cost more upfront, however, in the long term are much cheaper than buying disposable nappies. They can also be used for any other children you may have, further reducing the long-term financial burden to your family.

Other things to consider when making the choice is the potential health benefits of choosing cloth nappies. Disposables (unless you do a lot of research to choose a disposable with a minimal chemical load) contain dyes, perfumed fragrances, chlorines, and a plastic ingredient called Phthalates, all of which are a concern for the health of your baby.

Remember our skin is the largest organ in our body and readily absorbs chemicals placed in contact with it. Babies' skin is also a lot thinner, and they are rapidly growing, so these chemicals can have a greater impact on them.

The impact of disposables in our landfill system is huge, with disposables taking extremely long periods of time to break down. Solid faecal matter contained in disposable nappies should be disposed of into your toilet system, however, if it is not, it has the potential to escape into the ground water, causing contamination to our waterways.

Commercial Baby Wipes

Commercial baby wipes are only a recent invention. They have a huge environmental impact, as well as create sore and damaged skin, especially on sensitive babies. Most wet wipes are not degradable, so it could take 100 years or more for them to disappear from landfill.

Cleaning your baby's bottom when nappy changing is easy, cheap, and environmentally friendly when using face washers as an alternative to baby wipes. You can buy them in bulk and simply use some warm water. If more soiling has occurred, use 100% cotton wool balls, as non-organic varieties can contain synthetic fibres that are not biodegradable. Cotton growing is a crop that uses heavy amounts of pesticides, so residuals of that will be present unless organically grown. Also, purchase cotton wool made in your own country.

Set up your baby changing area in the nursery or laundry. In this area you would have a change mat, a large container with the cotton wool, a container of water (change regularly), and a small container for the rubbish. You will rarely need any creams and lotions to soothe sore and damaged skin.

A little bit of organisation and you will find this easy and more economical.

Purchasing products from your own country is so important. By doing this you are assisting your own economy, and you are reducing the pollution that is created from transporting long distances.

These are just some of the ways in which you can assist the environment, and in turn, the future for your baby.

It's time for us to look at the bigger picture of what we do on a daily basis and consider the consequences of our decisions. It's only by each of us making better choices that we can create the healthy world that we want our children to live in.

Bringing it all Together

EVEN THOUGH THE title of the book is aimed at women, as they are often the ones seeking information on bringing a baby into the world, my hope is that it will also be read by their partners and other members of their family. I wanted this book to be informative and easy to read. If we can support each other by passing on information and positive experiences, we can contribute towards a harmonious transition into motherhood.

As a society, we have had an interesting journey in history. In the past, life was a lot different than it is in our modern western world. History shows us that families and communities often grouped together for reasons of safety, support and the sharing of resources. Over time, living in communities diminished, with many populations now residing in single dwellings, living away from the extended family. We may feel safe and secure from threats such as turbulent weather and wild animals etc., however, as human beings, our basic need for company, sharing, and for support has not changed.

Before starting a family, a lot of our time is spent in the workplace, where we develop a level of support and community. However, for many women, feelings of isolation arise when they find themselves alone at home with a new baby, with their work community unavailable to them. Being aware of other women's experiences can help with understanding the importance of seeking out community beyond the work place before you bring a baby home. Setting up a strong network of support will help the transition to motherhood to be a positive experience.

STORY

Many years ago, on one of two visits to Vietnam, I observed how well the communities supported each other, despite a lack of resources and deficiencies in their medical system.

We were a group of people from the West, who came together to fundraise and assist in building a small postnatal room, supply medical and school supplies, concrete a school yard, and build toilets and a water filtration system for two small villages.

What we noticed most of all in these communities was that the community spirit was strong, and we were embraced by them completely.

When I arrived home, I noticed the lack of people in our suburban streets or seeing children playing in their yards. It seemed like such a contrast that I had never noticed before I travelled to Vietnam. It was a stark reminder to me of our isolation. A woman goes from being in a busy working environment where she feels in control and valued, to feeling alone in a house in the suburbs. Maybe her partner needs to return to work early, and her extended family are living interstate or overseas. This can be especially true with our new immigrant families. It can be quite a transition and shock for many to feel this isolation, along with the added pressures of needing to quickly become an expert in caring for a new baby. Thrown into this mix is tiredness and the physical changes that happen following pregnancy and birth. Often the pressures to return to the workforce early are considerable for financial reasons in a society that can value career over parenting.

On the second visit to Vietnam, a few of us were invited to be present at the birth of a baby. The baby had already been born when we arrived, however, it was such a privilege to see how the community were so excited about this new baby. Mother and baby were carried together in a colourful canopy sling through the streets to where the family lived, with quiet celebration happening around them. Everywhere we went there were people around who were friendly, happy, and ready to celebrate life. The feeling of community was incredibly strong. It was a privilege to participate in this experience.

Motherhood is an amazing and satisfying experience, one which is incredibly important in establishing the health and well-being of our future generations. It is important that our society cares about women and babies and embraces motherhood.

We should be questioning why a lot of women have negative experiences around birth and caring for their babies and young children. Are women feeling a lack of support when they become mothers? Are they experiencing feelings of isolation? With the cost of housing and living expenses, women are often forced back into the workforce when their babies are young. Other women find caring for babies and young children difficult due to social isolation, and can't wait to get back to work. Many women also suffer from the experience of postnatal depression.

When a woman makes a conscious choice, out of love, to become a mother, this is a powerful time, and motherhood needs to be returned to its rightful position as being one of the most important things that she will ever do in her life.

For most women in the modern world, pregnancy and motherhood is a choice. Within that choice, it is important to ask yourself what is your true motivation when deciding to become a mother (or parent)?

Some questions to consider are:
- ∞ Is my life, my maturity, my partnership and community solid and supportive?
- ∞ Do I have the wisdom within, that is needed, ready and willing to impart this to my child?

∞ Is my attitude towards motherhood one of obligation? Am I bringing a child into the world because, 'I want to get my family over and done with early so I can be free of children and still be young enough to enjoy myself', or 'I'll have my children later in life, so I can be free to establish my career, travel and have fun before I'm tied down', or 'after he or she is born, I'll be able to go back to work soon after the birth'.

Know that it is OK to choose not to be a parent. Be brave and honest within yourself if parenting is not for you. It is OK, in fact it's more than OK. A child who is brought up as an obligation has a difficult start in life. Their precious life deserves the very best of your time, attention and love. If you're not 100% available to do this, think twice, or three times, and then think again!

If the decision to become a mother has happened before you were ready, embracing the challenges can be more difficult, however, with plenty of support, it can work out just fine. If your circumstances mean going back into the work force early, planning and being organised will be helpful. If your family are not available to assist you with the care of your baby when you return to work, find a suitable carer, preferably prior to giving birth, so that you can establish a good relationship with them.

As a mother, be aware of taking on the legacy of our mothers and grandmothers in putting everyone's needs before our own. Running a household, being a mother, a partner, and attempting to do everything well, can create burnout in your life. In these modern times, working outside the home, in the workforce, can add extra stresses to your life. It is vitally important to remember to nurture yourself and create time for self-care. In doing so, you, your baby, your partner and others around you will experience the benefits.

Currently, we live in a world that often feels stressful. Whether it's our work life, meeting social, domestic, or family expectations and responsibilities, sitting in traffic jams, coping with fears that stem from world events, or feeling bombarded with huge amounts of information; all this stress creates problems in our biological systems. We know that releasing excessive amounts of the stress hormones, especially over long periods of time, suppresses our immune system, subsequently allowing us to become more susceptible to illnesses, as well as having a negative effect on the area of the brain (prefrontal cortex) that is designed to help with memory and learning.

In the year of 2021, life on our earth is unprecedented. We are globally experiencing what has been classified as a pandemic, and it is life changing for all humans on this planet in different ways. My hope is that we make this a time to reflect on our lives, know what our priorities are, shift many of our attitudes, and make positive changes in our lifestyle choices.

Bringing a baby into our life is incredibly special, has its challenges, but above all it is positively life changing, joyful, and a privilege. Enjoy every moment.

Acknowledgements

WHAT A JOURNEY writing a book is. After having written this book, when I pick up a book from now on, I will forever appreciate the efforts that go into its creation.

I always had an interest in writing and wrote small books as a child, however, it was not until a father said to me one day in my Lactation clinic that I should write a book, that the seed was sown. He was adamant that the information and practical tips that he received from me that day were very helpful for him to navigate through being a new dad, and that writing it down would be helpful to others.

Over the years, especially when I was travelling, I would sit down and scribble notes or type away on my iPad. As we sped through the countryside of Spain and France, I wrote down all the ideas that were gathering in my mind. It was an enjoyable exercise to undertake, especially when away from the busyness of everyday life.

One day I was talking to my good friend Sue, in an attempt to find a contact to help me put these writings together.

She said she would be able to help me herself, as she was equally as passionate about helping mothers and babies.

So, the journey began for us to put together the book you hold in your hands. I am forever grateful for your enthusiasm and commitment, Sue, as without your help, all the ideas may have ended up in a bag placed in a cupboard somewhere.

Becoming and being a mother is the most precious joy that I have ever experienced, and I wish to acknowledge my wonderful family – husband Frank and adult children Rachael, son in law Ryan, and Timothy. Your valuable help with adding ideas, editing text, and navigating through using technology has been invaluable.

I am most grateful to have chosen my career path as a Nurse, then as a Midwife. It is a privilege to be in the presence of other human beings when they are going through the most intimate of life experiences of birth, sickness, or passing over at the end of life. I am honoured to have been part of these experiences with so many.

I also wish to acknowledge the colleagues I have worked with over the years and the incredible support and friendships I have made along the way.

In writing the book, I wanted specific photos which were hard to find, so a lovely family came to the rescue. After an afternoon with Briar-Rose, Matthew, and their beautiful daughter, Isla, we had the photos we needed. A big thank you goes your way.

And to my good friend Phil, sharing your 'becoming a Dad' story came from the heart, and I appreciate you having shared that with us.

Most of all, I wish to acknowledge the newborn babies that come into the world. It is for the love of you that I do what I do, and if the pathway into this world is a little easier by writing this book, then I have done my job.

With love,

Julie

References, Resources and Insightful Information

Affirmations

These are positive statements that can help you to challenge and overcome self-sabotaging beliefs and negative thoughts.

Affirmations are like walking through a forest where there is no pathway. The more you walk back and forth through the forest, a pathway is created. This is the same as repeating affirmations. You develop new neural pathways (ways of thinking) within your brain. When you repeat them often, even if you don't initially believe them, they can make positive changes to your life.

Repeat These Each Day

I feel great joy when I am with my baby.

Mothering my baby is the most important thing I am doing right now.

I feel confident and empowered in my ability to care for my baby.

I am enough.

I am a wonderful mother.

I am happy and full of joy.

I am creating a beautiful life.

I radiate self confidence.

I breathe in the energy of love, and I breathe out negativity and doubt.

I take time to nurture my relationship with myself as I am worth it.

Aromatherapy Oils

The Fragrant Pharmacy written by Valerie Ann Worwood

Baby Products

Making Good Choices: https://www.productsafety.gov.au

Baby Wipes, Case Report Mary Wu Chang, MD, American Academy of Pediatrics, *Pediatrics*, Volume 133, Issue 2, February 2014.

Birth Information

Gentle Birth, Gentle Mothering – Sarah J. Buckley

Hypnobirthing Australia
https://hypnobirthingaustralia.com.au
A unique and comprehensive antenatal education program that builds knowledge confidence and tools that you need to birth calmly.

Delayed cord clamping

https://www.cochrane.org/CD004074/PREG_effect-timing-umbilical-cord-clamping-term-infants-mother-and-baby-outcomes

https://www.latrobe.edu.au/news/articles/2013/release/new-research-on-cord-clamping-in-babies

The Mode of Delivery and the Effect on the Diversity and Colonization Patterns of Gut Microbiota
https://pubmed.ncbi.nlm.nih.gov/27475754/

Breastfeeding

www.motherandbaby-workinginharmony.com.au
Short visual videos and other information. Simple and easy resources to assist you with techniques to enhance your breastfeeding and parenting experience.

Breastfeeding Matters – Maureen Minchin

Milk Matters, Infant Feeding and Immune Disorder – Maureen Minchin

Hanson L (2004) Immunology of Human Milk. How Breastfeeding Protects Babies

Saarinen UM (1982) Prolonged Breast Feeding

2010 Australian National Infant Feeding Survey
https://www.aihw.gov.au

Conscious parenting

The Biology of Belief – Bruce H. Lipton, Ph. D.

The Mind of Your Newborn Baby – David Chamberlain.

Pre-Parenting Nurturing Your Child From Conception – Thomas R. Verny, M.D., and Pamela Weintraub

Environment

Understanding Soil Health and a Healthy – Zac Bush, MD
https://www.youtube.com/watch?v=HL6OPzQe9Is&ab_channel=PRFCTEarthProject

Silent Spring – Rachel Carson
This book revolutionised the environmental movement in the last century resulting in the banning of the pesticide DDT and effecting many changes in the laws in regard to our land, air, and water.

Emotional Health

The E.F.T. Manual, Emotional Freedom Techniques – Dawson Church

The Science Behind Tapping, A Proven Stress Management Technique for the Mind and Body – Peta Stapleton, Ph. D.

The Tapping Solution, A Revolutionary System for Stress-Free Living – Nick Ortner

The Genie in Your Genes – Dawson Church, Ph. D. Epigenetic Medicine and the New Biology of Intention

How to Stop Worrying and Start Living – Dale Carnegie

Body Pleasure and the Origins of Violence – James W. Prescott
http://www.violence.de/prescott/bulletin/article.html

Fevers in children

www.rch.org.au/kidsinfo_sheets/Fever_in_children

Gut Health

"Eat Dirt! And Thrive", Zac Bush, MD.
https://www.youtube.com/watch?v=HL6OPzQe9Is

Health Outcomes

Health Outcomes Associated with Infant Feeding

Lucas A, Cole TJ 1990, Breast Milk and Necrotising Enterocolitis. *Lancet* 336(8730):1519–1523.

Victora CG, Horta BL, Loret De Mola C, Quevedo L, Pinheiro RT, Gigante DP, Goncalves H, Barros FC 2015, Association between breastfeeding and intelligence, educational attainment, and income at 30 years of age: a prospective birth cohort study from Brazil. *Lancet* 3:e199–205.

Immune system

Hanson L (2004) Immunology of Human Milk: How Breastfeeding Protects Babies

Forchielli ML. et al. (2005) The Role of Gut-Associated Lymphoid Tissues and Mucosal Defence.

Magnesium

Magnesium by Dr. Sandra Cabot

Nurturing from Conception

Pre-Parenting – Nurturing Your Child From Conception – Thomas R. Verny, M.D. and Pamela Weintraub

Alchemy of Intimacy: (Chapter 7, page 121)
"Modern parents are deluged with reams of conflicting information on how to raise children. But in the twenty-first century, findings from neurobiology point the way: relationships with a select group of adults, not sensory flooding, are the most important form of experience for the growing mind.

Parents, aware of the research, can apply these findings when bonding with their baby, positively imparting lifelong traits like empathy, independence and the ability to love. By meeting the physical, intellectual, emotional and moral needs of their children in predictable, empathetic and loving ways, parents help those children actualize their full human potential. When such children grow up, they will return to the world-many times over-the goodness they received."

Safe Sleeping

https://rednose.org.au/section/safe-sleeping

https://www.unicef.org.uk/babyfriendly/baby-friendly-resources/sleep-and-night-time-resources/caring-for-your-baby-at-night/

Dr Sarah Buckley MD – Gentle Birth, Gentle Mothering (chapter 13 page 247) Babies, Mothers, and the Science of Sharing Sleep

James J McKenna PhD – A Quick Guide to Safely Sleeping With Your Baby

Vitamins and Minerals

Butte NF et al. (2002) Nutrient Adequacy of Exclusive Breast-Feeding for the Term Infant During the First Six Months of Life.

Debier C (2007) Vitamin E During Pre and Postnatal Periods

Thomas MR et al. (1980) The Effects of Vitamin C, Vitamin B6, Vitamin B12, Folic Acid, Riboflavin, and Thiamine on the Breast Milk and Maternal Status of Well-Nourished Women at 6 months Postpartum

Wilson RD et al. (2007) Pre-Conceptional Vitamin Folic Acid Supplementation 2007.

Prentice A (2003) Micronutrients and the Bone Mineral Content of the Mother, Foetus and Newborn.

Vitamin K

Information on the Condition of Vitamin K Deficiency Bleeding (VKDB) in babies.

Vitamin K and the Newborn – Dr Sara Wickham

Prophylactic Vitamin K for Vitamin K Deficiency Bleeding in Neonates (Review)

https://www.cochranelibrary.com/cdsr/doi/10.1002/14651858.CD002776/full?highlightAbstract=prophylact%7Cprophylactic%7Ck%7Cvitamin

For further information and support go to my website

www.motherandbaby-workinginharmony.com.au

Here you will find references, resources and short educational videos on learning the skills to breastfeed.

www.ingramcontent.com/pod-product-compliance
Lightning Source LLC
Chambersburg PA
CBHW051537010526
44107CB00064B/2759